*A nostalgic look at*

# BIRMINGHAM TROLLEYBUSES

## 1922-51

**David Harvey**

Silver Link Publishing Ltd

This book is dedicated to my mother, Maisie Harvey,
who died before seeing the completed volume.

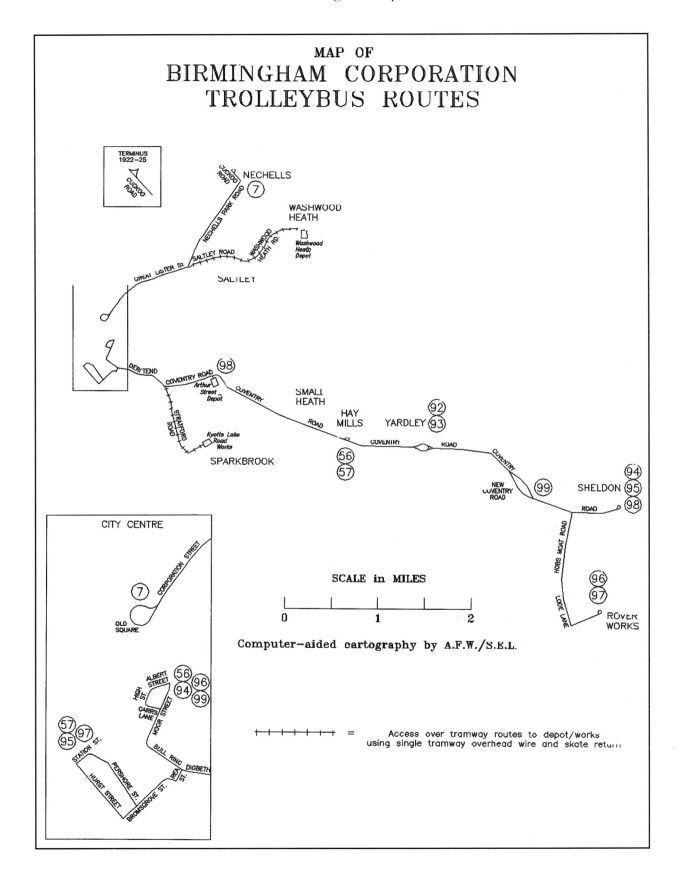

# MAP OF
# BIRMINGHAM CORPORATION
# TROLLEYBUS ROUTES

TERMINUS
1922-25
CUCKOO ROAD

CUCKOO ROAD
NECHELLS
⑦

WASHWOOD
HEATH

NECHELLS PARK ROAD

WASHWOOD HEATH RD.
Washwood
Heath
Depot

GREAT LISTER St.
SALTLEY ROAD
SALTLEY

DERITEND

COVENTRY ROAD
⑨⑧
Arthur
Street
Depot

COVENTRY

SMALL
HEATH

STRATFORD ROAD
Kyotts Lake
Road
Works

ROAD
HAY
MILLS
YARDLEY
⑨②
⑨③

COVENTRY
ROAD

SPARKBROOK

⑤⑥
⑤⑦

COVENTRY

⑨④
⑨⑤
⑨⑧

NEW
COVENTRY
ROAD
⑨⑨
SHELDON

ROAD

HOBS MOAT ROAD

CITY CENTRE

CORPORATION STREET

⑦
OLD
SQUARE

SCALE in MILES

0          1          2

Computer-aided cartography by A.F.W./S.E.L.

⑨⑥
⑨⑦
ROVER
WORKS

LODE LANE

ALBERT
STREET
⑤⑥
HIGH ST.
⑨④ ⑨⑥
⑨⑨
CARRS LANE

MOOR STREET

⑤⑦
⑨⑤
⑨⑦
STATION ST.

BULL RING    DIGBETH

PERSHORE ST.
REA ST.

HURST STREET
BROMSGROVE ST.

┼┼┼┼┼┼┼ = Access over tramway routes to depot/works
using single tramway overhead wire and skate return

# CONTENTS

# BIBLIOGRAPHY

To mention all the sources used in this book would produce an exceptionally long list; this is not intended to be comprehensive, but includes those that were used most frequently.

Joyce, J., King, J. S. & Newman, A. G. *British Trolleybus Systems* (Ian Allan, 1986)
Keeley, M., Russell, M. & Gray, P. *Birmingham City Transport* (TPC, 1977)
Lumb, G. *British Trolleybus 1911-1972* (Ian Allan, 1995)
Mayou, C. A., Stanford, J. D. & Barker, T. *Birmingham Corporation Tramways* (TPC, 1982)
Mayou, C. A. 'Birmingham Tram and Trolleybus overhead' (unpublished paper)
York, F. W. *The Trolleybuses of Birmingham* (BTS, 1971)

Various magazines including: *Buses Illustrated*; *Modern Tramways*; *Tramway and Railway World*; *Transport World*; *Trolleybus Magazine*

The numerous books available on the local history of Birmingham include:
Price, V. J. *Birmingham Cinemas*
*Birmingham Theatres, Concert and Music Hall*
Skipp, V. *Victorian Birmingham*
*Developing Birmingham 1889-1989*

In addition a number of most useful books on cars were used, the best being the 'British Cars' series by Piet Olyslager, published by Frederick Warne.

© David Harvey 1997
Route maps © J. C. Gillham
General system map © Stan Letts and Arthur Whitehouse

First published in November 1997

British Library Cataloguing in Publication Data

A catalogue record for this book is available from the British Library.

ISBN 1 85794 069 5

Silver Link Publishing Ltd
Unit 5
Home Farm Close
Church Street
Wadenhoe
Peterborough  PE8 5TE
Tel  (01832) 720440
Fax  (01832) 720531
e-mail: pete@slinkp-p.demon.co.uk

Printed and bound in Great Britain

# ACKNOWLEDGEMENTS

THE MAIN DIFFICULTY in producing this volume was that the Birmingham trolleybus system closed in 1951. While the tramcar fleet was well-known and in post-war years very comprehensively photographed, the same could not be said about the trolleybus fleet. Always taking a minor role in the road transport scene in the city, few enthusiastic photographers went to the Nechells route, while the Coventry Road service was only 'discovered' when it was doomed to closure. I am therefore indebted to all those photographers who visited the system, took photographs and allowed me to use their work.

The aim of this volume is to take a journey through time along both the trolleybus routes in order to view the trolleybuses in their transportational, historical and social context. This volume was a long time in the planning and development stages and unfortunately a number of these elderly gentlemen have not lived to see the completed work.

My thanks are extended to that doyen of tram photographers, the late Arthur Camwell, the late Bob Mack and to the late Leslie Perkins, who took photographs of the Nechells route in the early days of the Second World War. Thanks also to John Eades who allowed me to use photographs from the late Stanley Eades's collection, and to the late Fred Lloyd whose paper negatives were such an unusual and valuable find.

Special acknowledgment is due to Peter Drake of the Local Studies Department of Birmingham Central Reference Library for giving me unrestricted access to their photographic collection. I am also obliged to the *Birmingham Post & Mail* for allowing me to use the press cuttings from the *Birmingham Mail* concerning the closure of the trolleybus system in June 1951. My appreciation is also due to John Whybrow's Photographic Studio of Sparkbrook, for allowing me entry to their splendid archive of scenes of Birmingham; this enabled me to use a number of previously undiscovered trolleybus photographs.

I must also give special recognition to Ray Wilson, whose excellent and often unusual photographs of Birmingham trolleybuses form such an integral part of this volume.

I am indebted to Clarence Carter and Arnold Richardson of Photobus who provided me with the colour prints, and to Stan Letts whose hand-tinted colour prints adorn the book jacket.

I am most grateful to Alan Cross, John Edgington, Michael Rooum and Peter Yeomans who willingly offered their photographs for inclusion in this book. Roy Marshall was particularly helpful as his extensive collection of early trolleybus photographs proved a most valuable source of material.

Although better known as the authority on Black Country trams, Stanley Webb allowed me the privilege of extracting from his extensive collection of previously unpublished Birmingham trolleybus photographs a number of prints that are included in this volume.

Malcolm Keeley let me use his collection of large-format prints while John Hughes allowed me to use his collection of trolleybus pictures and also those taken by the late Cliff Brown.

More specialised acknowledgements must be given to a number of friends and enthusiasts who helped in other ways in the production of this book. John Gillham has once again graciously allowed me to dissect one of his splendid maps, in order this time to show the Nechells and Coventry Road trolleybus routes in detail. Also I am once again appreciative of the hard work of Arthur Whitehouse, ably assisted by Stan Letts, who produced the precise computer generated general layout map of the Birmingham trolleybus system.

Phillip Groves was, as usual, very informative about the electrical equipment fitted to the trolleybus fleet, and Geoff Lumb gave me a considerable amount of information about the early trackless trolley fleet.

One of the most illuminating sources of factual information were the BCT Trolleybus Record Cards. The analysis of these provided a considerable amount of hitherto unknown information about overhauls, withdrawal dates and mileage data. I am extremely happy to record my appreciation to my colleagues in the Birmingham Transport Historical Group and to Peter Jacques of the Kithead Trust for giving me free access to this valuable data resource.

Barry Ware also allowed me to use his extensive ticket collection and explained the intricacies of BCT ticket colours and denominations.

The 'past and present' photographs, using the preserved ex- Birmingham City Transport Crossley DD42/7, 2489 (JOJ 489), were taken on a extremely hot Sunday in July 1996. Had it not been for the patience and sweat of Barry Ware, who was driving the bus, the excellent results would have not been possible. The trolleybus blind used in the Crossley, which adds to the authenticity of the 'then and now' scenes, was kindly lent to me by Mac Cooper of the Aston Manor Transport Museum. It is also worth recording that had it not been for the helpful Security Supervisor, the photographs within the confines of the Rover Works at Lode Lane would not have been possible.

A word of thanks is also due to the helpful, anonymous member of the personnel department of A. D. Wimbush, who sent me a most useful account of the history of the company and its present-day production figures.

Special thanks are also due to Wilf Watters of Online Video who helped me to produce the stills from the 1930 film of the Guy BTX running on the Nechells route.

I wish to pay thanks to the 'backroom boys', who helped me to produce photographs from prints when the negatives had been lost. Ray Marshall at Newman College, Birmingham, worked miracles with numerous prints, while Roger Carpenter produced some superb results from indifferent negatives.

This volume, however, could not have been produced

without reference to the original publication about Birmingham's trolleybuses. In 1971 Fred York produced the then definitive work, *The Trolleybuses of Birmingham*, published by the British Trolleybus Society. This is a quite splendid source of information and only the passage of time and the subsequent emergence of new material has caused this excellent standard reference book to require updating.

I am most grateful to Derek Potter of the BTHG, as not only did he proof-read the manuscript, but also allowed me to use photographs from his extensive collection. He also added a considerable amount of information to the text as well as providing electrical drawings and trolleybus blinds. I would also wish to express my appreciation to Richard Weaver and to Barry Ware who both proof-read the draft copy and offered constructive help and suggestions.

I would also like to acknowledge the enormous support and encouragement given to me by my wife, Diana, who offered moral support when the going got tough, who proof-read the very first embryonic draft and who offered both technical and grammatical advice.

A special acknowledgment that I must give is to a transport photographer who never took a photograph of a Birmingham trolleybus. Norman Glover, whose excellent tram photographs appear in the three earlier tram volumes, died in December 1996 without seeing the book published, but whose advice and encouragement was invaluable.

I am also extremely grateful to the staff of the 'Waggon & Horses', Oldbury and 'The Farmer's Arms', Mathry, for their hospitality and patience while this book was in production.

Finally, a special thanks is due to Peter Townsend and Will Adams of Silver Link Publishing Ltd for their equanimity and fortitude during the long gestation of this volume.

Acknowledging everyone who has helped me to produce this book is a little like a tearful and drawn-out acceptance speech at an Oscar ceremony, so if I have forgotten anyone, I sincerely apologise, and to all of you who have helped, I trust that you consider the effort worthwhile as you read this *Nostalgic Look at Birmingham Trolleybuses*.

**David Harvey**
**Dudley, West Midlands**

# INTRODUCTION

THIS FOURTH BOOK about Birmingham in the 'Nostalgic look at. . .' series looks at the city's trolleybuses, which are a method of public transport that has been largely forgotten by its citizens, enthusiasts and transport historians.

The basic facts are that there were two unconnected routes, to Nechells and along Coventry Road, which at a maximum covered some 10.18 miles. Birmingham Corporation trolleybuses operated for over 28 years using 114 trolleybuses; the maximum fleet strength reached 90 vehicles for about two days at the end of February 1940, which made the system the 16th largest of the 50 trolleybus operators in Britain.

Birmingham was one of this country's pioneering trolleybus operators, being the 14th system to open. The Nechells trolleybus route began operation on 27 November 1922 with a fleet of top-covered double-deck Railless trolleybuses. From the city centre terminus in Old Square, the journey of 2.44 miles, over what had previously been an unremunerative tram route through areas of heavy industry and Victorian housing, had seemed an enormous gamble, but by January 1923 there had been an increase in receipts of just over 51 per cent. Prospective trolleybus operators came to the city to view the success story and for two or three years Birmingham's trolleybuses were at the forefront of this type of vehicle operation.

It might therefore have been assumed that the General Manager, Alfred Baker, would have consolidated this initial success and converted more tram routes to the new 'Trolley Omnibuses'. Unfortunately the expansion of trolleybuses into other parts of the city was not considered a priority after the mid-1920s. Tram route extensions continued until 1928, but, unlike in cities such as Liverpool and Sheffield, this growth then came to a halt. The municipal housing estates opened up at the edge of Birmingham were left to the increasingly reliable and more manoeuvrable petrol-engined and slightly later oil-engined buses.

As the original Railless fleet became due for replacement, having tried numerous demonstration vehicles, Birmingham became instrumental in persuading Leyland Motors to build trolleybuses. GEC, the Witton-based electrical component manufacturer, was keen to break into the trolleybus traction-motor business. With the cognisance of the Corporation, Leyland Motors developed prototype two-axle and three-axle trolleybuses, both of which were demonstrated on the Nechells route. This led to Leyland obtaining its first trolleybus order; these were the unique half-cab two-axle Leylands for the Nechells route.

The first six-wheelers were bought in 1932. These were five AEC 663Ts and gave the Department the opportunity to operate trolleybuses that were physically larger and able to carry more passengers.

Possible opportunities to expand the trolleybus system were not taken until 1934 when they were used to replace the ageing tramcars on the worn-out track of the Yardley route. The purchase of 50 new vehicles was at the time the largest order ever placed for a batch of trolleybuses in this country. The real gamble was that they were the first production Leyland six-wheeled chassis to be manufactured, and additionally they had some of the earliest metal-framed bodies built on trolleybuses. These were supplied by the Saltley-based Metropolitan-Cammell Carriage & Wagon Company.

The Yardley route was extended to the city boundary in Sheldon in July 1936. This was the only part of the system that ran into 1930s suburbia. It was an area of semi-detached houses with bay-windows, wide grass verges and concrete roads, which somehow epitomised trolleybus operation. Further new vehicles were required, although BCT reverted to Leyland four-wheeled trolleybuses for this extension. In 1939, when the half-cab Leyland trolleybuses of 1932 were becoming due for replacement, BCT again opted for Leyland four-wheelers.

The Second World War caused enormous disruption. The Nechells service was suspended from October 1940 because of blackout regulation infringements occurring on journeys to and from Washwood Heath depot over the tram tracks. This necessitated the use of a skate attached to the tram rails, which caused flashes, and it was thought that these might be visible to enemy aircraft at night.

This loss of mileage was partially compensated for by the only trolleybus route extension in the country authorised under the Emergency Powers Act of 1939. This was to the Rover Works in Lode Lane, Solihull, and added nearly 1½ miles to the remaining route along Coventry Road. It also gave the trolleybuses a long section of route outside the city boundary, although other services had gone further, such as the former Black Country Company tramcar routes 'inherited' by BCT, which had been closed in April and September 1939.

Despite the efficiency of the trolleybuses in the city, Birmingham, originally wedded to the tramcar, passed them over in favour of the diesel-engined bus. The high standards of maintenance of the overhead, the excellent condition of the trolleybus fleet and the infrastructure became unimportant! The intense service requirements on both trolleybus routes, especially along Coventry Road, where a 2-minute headway was operated, became only a minor consideration.

Once the decision was made in 1948 to scrap the trams, a fleet of by now 74 trolleybuses amongst a bus fleet of 1,800-plus was simply not viable. When it closed, with minimal ceremony, at the end of June 1951, it was the 13th system to be abandoned, the first post-war trolleybus system closure and the first to be outlived by the trams that it should have replaced!

This book shows the trolleybus in its geographical, historical and social context. It was a child of the 1920s, blossoming in the '30s, losing face because of its old-fashioned ideas, then having a renaissance in the '40s and prematurely dying in the '50s. The photographs, many of which have never been published before, capture the trolleybuses during their lifetime in the city.

Birmingham's trolleybuses were really never more than a glorified experiment; never really wanted, they did not reach their full potential. In many ways the system was strangely conservative and old-fashioned, never using automatic overhead frogs and retaining trolley-wheels when trolleyskates were regarded as the norm nearly everywhere else after the mid-1930s. Yet it was at the forefront of vehicle development. Although the trolleybuses always had bodies with 'the Birmingham look', beneath the surface of thick window pillars, moulded panelling and straight staircases, the Birmingham vehicles were always up to date with current trolleybus technology.

The Birmingham trolleybus is shown in its setting by taking pictorial journeys along both the 7 route to Nechells and 'down the Coventry Road' to the city boundary and Lode Lane. Hopefully these excursions will revive memories of those fortunate enough to have seen them and travelled on Birmingham's 'Silent Service'.

# A HISTORY OF
# ═ BIRMINGHAM'S TROLLEYBUS ═
# SYSTEM

## The pioneering trackless years, 1922-1930

THE ORIGINS OF Birmingham's trolleybus system can be found in the enforced lack of maintenance on the tram network during the First World War.

The electric tram service to Nechells was one of 16 routes opened in the city on Tuesday 1 January 1907. The new service was given the letter N on a red background, and in 1915 was numbered 7. It replaced the last horse-tram route in the city, which was the City of Birmingham Tramways Company service from Albert Street via Curzon Street and Bloomsbury Street to Long Acre in Nechells.

After the CBT lease expired on 31 December 1906, the mainly single-track route was operated by either open-topped Brill-trucked cars of the 21 or 221 Classes, or the later 71 Class of top-covered UEC-bodied four-wheelers. The route was never very profitable, reflecting the fact that CBT had not converted the route to electric traction before its lease had expired.

By 1921, with the Nechells track in a poor state of repair, it was decided to experiment with 'trackless trolleys'. A delegation from the Transport Committee led by the General Manager was sent to Bradford, where they assessed the two experimental top-covered double-deck trolleybuses, numbered 521 and 522, that were being successfully operated.

As a result of this visit, the decision was made to go ahead with the conversion of the Nechells tram service to trolleybus operation. An order was placed with the Railless Company of Rochester, Kent, in August 1921 to supply 12 42hp double-deck LF-type chassis, which were fabricated by Short Brothers. The body order was placed with Charles Roe of Crossgates, Leeds, for top-covered, outside-staircase, 51-seater bodies at a total cost of £36,000. These 12 trolleybuses were the first double-deck bodies that Roe had manufactured; the order caused severe financial problems, resulting in the need to refinance the company as Charles H. Roe (1923) Ltd. After being towed to Birmingham, some of the first to arrive had broken windows due to having hit low branches; later vehicles were delivered with protective tarpaulins covering the upper saloon windows.

The application to replace the trams with trolleybuses was granted *after* the order for the vehicles was placed. The Birmingham Corporation Act 1922, Part IV, subtitled 'Trolley Vehicles, Tramways and Omnibuses' overcame the reluctance and objections of the Board of Trade to allow top-covered double-deck buses. In addition to the vehicles, the rest of the Nechells conversion included £15,000 for the removal of the tram track, and alterations to the overhead wires, which cost another £3,000. The overhead was spaced 13 inches apart on the Nechells route as opposed to the later 18 inches. The new route was 2.44 miles from Old Square to the Nechells terminus at the junction of Cuckoo Road and Long Acre.

The Railless trolleybuses were numbered 1 to 12 (OK 4823-4834), and were an immediate success with the passengers. There was a 4-minute headway on the service with an average of seven stops per mile and an average speed of 10 miles per hour. In the first eight weeks receipts had risen from £2,589 to £3,914, which represented a 51.7 per cent increase, while the mileage had risen over the same period by 37.5 per cent.

Alfred Baker pronounced: 'The Trolley Omnibus gives the passengers a most comfortable ride . . . they run with extreme smoothness and are practically noiseless . . . it is this beautiful riding factor which has done so much to popularise the Trolley Omnibus in Birmingham.'

For a time, with the General Manager extolling the virtues of the trolley omnibus, it seemed that Birmingham Corporation might replace further loss-making tram routes. But nothing happened!

The introduction of the 12 Raillesses placed Birmingham at the forefront of British trolleybus develop-ment. Deputations from Chesterfield, Darlington, Oldham, Newcastle and Wigan visited the Nechells route in order to assess the suitability or otherwise of the new form of traction for their respective towns, with Mr Baker offering professional advice by surveying some of these systems.

One permanent dividend of the top-covered trolleybus fleet was that an AEC 503 bus chassis was temporarily fitted with a top cover in July 1924. This was considered to be so successful that all future double-deck deliveries, starting with AEC 503, 101 (OL 8100), were fitted with top-covers. Bus fleets around the country, not only those in Birmingham, owed a considerable debt to the original, trail-blazing Railless trolleybuses as they promoted the acceptance of top-covered double-deckers in Britain.

In 1923 a single-deck AEC 602, based on the 'S'-type motor bus chassis and fitted with a Hora B36R body, was demonstrated between 17 August and the end of October. It was painted red and cream, given the fleet number 13 and registered OL 994. Only six 602 chassis were built and this vehicle appears to have led something of a mysterious existence after its period in Birmingham, apparently being sold to Mexborough & Swinton in 1924.

On 10 April 1924 the next vehicle was delivered. Numbered 13 (OL 4636), it was the only trolleybus built by the Electro-Magnetic Brake Company of West Bromwich. It was powered by two English Electric DK85A 42hp motors, which drove the rear wheels by way of two propeller shafts outside the chassis frame. This enabled the chassis frame to be extremely low and the rear platform to be just one step from the kerb-side. The Roe H28/20R low-height body was the first in the fleet to have a totally enclosed staircase - it was years before its time!

It ran until 31 March 1926, by which time it had covered 20,894 miles. It was returned to EMB on 29 June 1928. It is a great shame that this company did not have the resources to develop the design further.

In 1926 the last trackless vehicles were added to the fleet. The first three were Railless LFs, built with Short bodies; these were numbered 14-16 (ON 2825-2827). The fourth chassis was exhibited at the 1926 Olympia Show in full Birmingham City Transport (BCT) livery, but was rejected by the General Manager as it had a foot-controller (accelerator pedal), which was not standard in the Birmingham fleet. As a result the trolleybus was sold to Nottingham Corporation, where it became their number 10 (TO 5010). The three Birmingham vehicles were previously thought to be AEC 607s, but they were ordered through the Railless Company. It is believed that the chassis frames may have been manufactured on behalf of the Railless company by AEC.

The final 'solid-tyred' vehicle was an AEC 607 chassis. It had a Vickers H26/26RO body and entered service on 3 March 1926. Despite the debacle with the Olympia Show vehicle, this trolleybus did have foot-controllers! It was given the fleet number 17 (ON 3261), and made up the Nechells route trolleybus fleet that would provide an efficient service for the next six years. The trail-blazing 'trackless' fleet increased the service frequency after the withdrawal of the trams and ensured that the previous loss-making service was making a regular profit.

It was a little unfortunate for BCT that during the three-year period after the delivery of No 17 in 1926, the 'track-less-tram' concept was replaced by modern 'electric buses', such as those being manufactured by Guy Motors of Wolverhampton and Karrier in Huddersfield. Within seven years the pioneering vehicles of 1922 had become an anachronism! The Birmingham fleet that had been at the vanguard of trolley vehicle evolution in Britain had been overtaken by design and operational progress.

## Demonstrators and the second generation, 1930-1932

By 1930 it was becoming obvious that the solid-tyred Railless fleet was approaching the end of its life span. Most of the 1-12 Class had already run just over 200,000 miles and had received two overhauls, while the three Railless LFs (14-16) and the AEC 607 (17), while barely four years old, were very old-fashioned-looking, with their outside staircases and solid tyres.

The need for replacement vehicles was becoming important, so Guy Motors was approached with a view to examining its six-wheeled trolleybuses. In the event two buses were demonstrated. The first, numbered 18 (UK 8341), was a BTX model, powered by a Rees 60hp motor and fitted with a Guy H27/26R body. This was the first trolleybus to have an enclosed staircase, and all subsequent BCT trolleybuses had this feature. No 18 was always supposed to have been driven under its own power from Wolverhampton to Birmingham via Dudley, but the tale is apocryphal as the trolleybus was towed behind a Guy Motors lorry along Birmingham New Road! It entered service on 22 February 1930 and was used in a publicity film by Guy Motors; it remained in Birmingham for 17 months, during which time it ran over 19,000 miles.

The second Guy vehicle was a RTX type fitted with a Rees Roturbo 75hp regenerative motor. It was numbered 19, and although it only stayed in the city for one week in April 1931, it was registered in Birmingham as OG 9886. It also had a Guy H27/26R body, but had a Birmingham-style straight staircase. Despite this design feature, which was to be such an important characteristic of BCT bodies, OG 9886 never ran in revenue service!

After their stay in the city both of these trolleybuses were stored by Guys before being sold to Llanelly & District in January 1935. OG 9886 became Llanelly's 16, while UK 8341 was re-registered as TH 5167 and received the fleet number 17. They ran in Llanelly until 1945.

During the Depression years, the need to develop local industry meant that the Witton-based General Electric Co Ltd came to an agreement with Leyland Motors to supply suitably modified electric traction motors. Leyland had only dabbled in supplying chassis frames, based on the 'Lion' PLSC1, to English Electric in 1928 and 1929; these were supplied to Bradford Corporation as single-decker trolleybuses.

The first trolleybus to be constructed was known as the TBD1. Completed in January 1931, it was based on a modified Leyland 'Titan' chassis and fitted with a GEC WT25 65hp motor and a GEC FA3B controller (this last designation was for many years attributed falsely to the chassis type). It carried a Short Brothers L24/24R body to Leyland design and, with its half-cab and polished radia-tor, it looked like a normal petrol bus with poles coming out of its roof!

After being tested on the recently opened South Lancashire system, it arrived in Birmingham as the new 19 (OV 1175), entering service on 20 May 1931. It ran inter-mittently until the end of August, having recorded 2,167 miles on the Nechells route, before being returned to Leyland. After this period of demonstration it reappeared in Chesterfield before being converted to a petrol-engined bus and being sold to Jersey Motor Traction, registered J 1199. It survived the German occupation of the Channel Islands and is preserved today as MJX 222J, although it is very difficult to recognise it as a trolleybus.

The demonstration was considered to be a success, and as a result an order was placed with Leyland in the sum-mer of 1931, originally for ten four-wheeled TBD1 trolley-buses, although this was amended in October to 11. This was the first production batch of Leyland trolleybuses to be built. It was no real surprise that the need to support local industry favoured the Leyland/GEC combination, and for this reason the body order was placed with John Buckingham, the Birmingham body-builder. Unfortunately this Bradford Street-based company fell victim to the depression, and the order was transferred to Short Brothers; this company was building bodies on the 444-483 (OV 4444-4483) batch of AEC 'Regent' 661s, which were delivered to BCT between August and November 1931.

The Leyland trolleybuses again looked like the standard Birmingham motor bus of the day; they continued the half-cab design of OV 1175 and even retained the chrome-plated radiator with a filler cap! The vehicles were equipped with magnificent brass-rimmed headlights and side-lights at the front, and had the usual number of four destination boxes. The trolleybuses were already overweight, and when No 1 was submitted for its type test, it failed the mandatory tilt-test. As a result the head-lights were removed, the upper saloon seating was reduced by one, and all the destination gear in all four displays was taken out. Until about 1937, these trolleybus-es only displayed paper stickers that read NECHELLS instead of the rather short linen blind that, as well as the other three displays, usually showed NECHELLS 7.

The new trolleybuses were numbered 1-3/5-7/9-11/13/15, with matching registrations starting with OV 4001, etc. The 11 trolleybuses entered service from Washwood Heath tram depot on 2-5 February 1932, over a month after the ill-fated tilt-test with No 1. The missing fleet numbers, 4 and 8, were then still carried by the last two of the 1-12 batch of 1922 Raillesses to be repainted, which remained in service until 31 August 1932. For their last months they were numbered 13 and 15 respectively. Of the four other members of the original fleet, both Railless 14 and the solitary AEC 607, 17, also remained in service until the end of August 1932, while Railless 16 ran until March 1932.

The old Raillesses of the 1-12 class each ran over a quarter of a million miles in service, while the newer quartet managed around 100,000 miles each.

The final trolleybus to be demonstrated in 1931, when the Leyland prototype was still in Birmingham, was a Guy BT. It had a Guy 60hp motor and a Guy L24/24R body to

Park Royal design, and arrived in May carrying the fleet number 20 (OV 1194). It was placed in service on 20 May 1931 and was sent back to Guys 11 days later. Very little was known about this vehicle until a Roy Marshall photograph turned up of a Guy 'Arab' II chassis registered MRF 634 with Trumans of Shirebrook; the oddly proportioned body was that from the 1931 Guy trolleybus. After its short period of demonstration it had been stored by Guys until 1934, when it was converted to a petrol-engined Guy 'Arab'. After being re-chassised in 1946, the ungainly MRF 634 ran until 1949, when the aged former trolleybus body was replaced by a Unity (Barnsley British Co-op) C32F single-deck body, in which guise it lasted until withdrawal in 1959.

The opening of Perry Barr bus garage on 16 February 1932 was the occasion when the General Manager, A. C. Baker, announced the placing of an order for five new six-wheeled trolleybuses. These were AEC 663T chassis, with English Electric 80hp motors and Brush H33/25R bodies, and were needed to supplement the Leyland TBD1s on the Nechells route. An AEC 663T demonstrator, mounted on 663T002, with an experimental five-bay-construction body built by English Electric, was inspected by the Transport Department on 28 June 1932 and obviously created a good impression. This vehicle, or at least parts of its chassis, returned as number 16, re-bodied and with a new chassis number of 663T070. The quintet entered service between 19 August and 8 September 1932 and the Birmingham trolleybus system settled down for a short period of stability.

## Coventry Road problems and opening

By 1932 the state of the track along the main arterial Coventry Road was in need of renewal. An estimated £27,870 worth of track replacement between Cattell Road and the terminus at Yardley was required on a route that, despite a nature different from the Nechells situation of ten years earlier, presented similar problems. It too was disappointingly unremunerative and was operating elderly open-balconied four-wheel trams. The discussion as to what to do with the Coventry Road route was finally resolved at the July 1932 meeting of the Transport Committee when it was decided to accept the General Manager's view that trolleybuses should replace the trams.

Within weeks the euphoria of that decision and the entry into service of the new AECs was dashed. The Minister of Transport, the appropriately named Mr P. J. Pybus, announced in August 1932 the setting up of the Conference of Rail and Road Transport under the Chairmanship of Sir Arthur Salter. Its aim was to arrive at a fair basis for equal competition between rail and road transport. This was a potentially damaging document to any operator of trolleybuses as it proposed to increase the licence duty on an individual trolleybus from £96 to £554 16s per annum on a vehicle of between 56 and 64 seats. This would nullify any advantage that the trolleybus, obtaining its electrical power quite cheaply from the Corporation Electricity Department, might have had over the motorbus. The result was that no operator was pre-

pared to develop any new routes until the Budget announcement in April 1933, although the significance of the Salter Report is hardly mentioned in contemporary influences on other trolleybus systems that were being developed such as Huddersfield and Portsmouth. In the event, the proposals of the Salter Committee were never even mentioned by the Chancellor of the Exchequer!

The track along Coventry Road had deteriorated further by the time that the Transport Committee, at its first post-Budget meeting in May 1933, made the decision to proceed with the Yardley tram-to-trolleybus conversion. The service was converted to trolleybuses under the terms of the Birmingham Corporation Act of 1922. The undertaking was allowed to 'with the consent of the Minister of Transport and subject to such conditions as he may impose, use trolley vehicles along any road in the city along which they are authorised to construct or use tramways'.

The time lost between the decision to convert to trolleybuses and the go-ahead being given meant that, crucially, eight months of stagnation at a vital time had lost the trolleybus the chance to develop even more in the city. The opportunity to make the eastern tram routes a corridor for the trolleybus had disappeared when the Bolton Road tram route was abandoned on 4 February 1930. This would have enabled the trolleybuses to have run along the former 22 tram route in Bordesley Park Road, via Bolton Road and Byron Road to the terminus just short of the BSA factory gates on the corner of Oldknow Road. About 600 yards of overhead would have had to be erected in Oldknow Road, alongside Small Heath Park, to rejoin the proposed Coventry Road trolleybus wires and form a significant loop service that would have also benefited the Singer car factory.

A further nail in the coffin of the Birmingham trolleybus was the arrival of a demonstrator from Transport Vehicles (Daimler) of Coventry. It arrived on 27 November 1933 and left on 15 December. The significance of this motorbus, KV 1396, was the combination for the first time in a double-deck Daimler chassis of a Wilson pre-selector gearbox and fluid flywheel, as already found in the petrol-engined CP6 chassis, with a Gardner 5LW 7.0-litre diesel engine. It was fitted with a six-bay Brush body. This vehicle offered economy, manoeuvrability and an ease of operation with which the trolleybus could not compete. Although it was not realised at the time, the new Coventry Road trolleybuses, before they were even delivered, would be relegated to a minor role in the city; the trolleybus versus motorbus debate had already been lost at the very moment of triumph!

A Leyland TTBD1 six-wheeled demonstrator, TJ 939, arrived in the city on 11 March 1933 and spent the next five months running along the Nechells route, although it apparently did not enter revenue service despite running 5,258 miles. It was hired at a rate of 3½d per mile and was used as a test-bed for the GEC electric motor as well as for training drivers for the as yet to be opened Yardley service.

This bus was sufficiently successful that in May 1933 A. C. Baker placed an order for 50 six-wheeled Leyland TTBD2 trolleybuses, powered by GEC WT25 65hp motors. These cost the undertaking £95,000 and differed from TJ 939 by having their traction motors placed between the chassis frame instead of over the front axle. This enabled the body height to be lower on the production vehicles, which would be an advantage at Bordesley railway bridge. The bodies were 58-seat metal-framed structures built by the Metropolitan-Cammell Carriage & Wagon Company (MCCW). The previous batch of trolleybuses had quite similar-looking composite bodies built by Brush Coachworks of Loughborough; these had proved very satisfactory but Brush could not supply metal-framed bodies at the time the tenders were being invited. By purchasing metal-framed bodies from Metro-Cammell, the Corporation was also supporting Birmingham-based industry at the time of the Depression.

These 50 Metro-Cammell-bodied Leyland TTBD2s constituted the largest single order ever placed for trolleybuses in the UK up to this time. The batch of trolleybuses was numbered 17-66 (OC 1117-1166), just failing by four months to get a three-letter registration mark. 'OC' was issued in late 1933, out of sequence, as the last two-letter registration issued by the Birmingham Motor Taxation Office. They were not the first metal-framed double-deck trolleybuses, as 15 AEC/EEs had been bodied by Metro-Cammell as its contract number 31 and delivered to the Nottinghamshire & Derbyshire Traction Company in 1933; the BCT ones had contract number 36. In addition, the size of the Birmingham order would be easily eclipsed within two years when London Transport's first large orders for AEC 664Ts were delivered.

At the end of October 1933 one of the new trolleybuses, almost certainly the first one, 17 (OC 1117), was seen in the Old Square painted all-over in grey primer and carrying trade-plates 098 VP. It was devoid of all markings and was initially used for clearance tests, although quite why it was being pushed around Old Square remains something of a mystery.

The new trolleybuses were delivered from Metro-Cammell from mid-November, and after being tested over the Nechells route they were towed to Perry Barr garage for storage. The Coventry Road overhead was completed by December 1933, and in the week after Christmas driver training took place on the unopened Yardley route using one of the AEC 663Ts from Washwood Heath depot. Prior to the opening of the service, AEC 663T 13 (OJ 1013) gave members of the Transport Committee (and a quantity of sandbags to simulate a full load) a demonstration run to Yardley in pouring rain.

By Sunday 4 January 1934 the fleet of new trolleybuses was ensconced in Coventry Road depot ready for the new service to begin, which it did, without ceremony, the following day. Coventry Road depot lost to other depots 46 of its Brill 21E-truck four-wheelers and ex-CBT cars at the time of the conversion, but for the first time after a tram conversion, ominously, a few tramcars were scrapped.

The conversion from trams to trolleybuses was seen as a great success! Increased headway to just 2 minutes, higher revenue and a new state-of-the-art fleet of vehicles offered the public a fast, reliable and comfortable mode of transport along Coventry Road for the first time in many years. The only problems on the new 5.23-mile route were minor ones with the Leyland trolleybuses. They were at first prone to the cutting out of their electri-

cal contactors, and faults in the dynamo causing a spate of flat batteries.

Only one more six-wheeler was delivered to the undertaking after the opening of the Yardley route. This was a Sunbeam MS2, with a BTH 201-type 90hp motor. It was fitted with a very early metal-framed MCCW H31/28R body, which had the MCCW contract number 24. Exhibited at the 1933 Commercial Motor Show in full BCT livery, it was delivered to Birmingham on 9 February 1934 as 67 (OC 6567), but only ran until 24 March before being returned to Sunbeam; it was never owned by Birmingham. The vehicle was subsequently sold to Wolverhampton, where it was numbered 222 and ran until April 1949.

## Out into suburbia

The absorption of Sheldon into the city in 1931 and the construction of well over 1,000 council houses in the area within five years made the extension of the trolleybus route from Yardley a matter of some priority. Under the terms of the Birmingham Corporation Act of 1935, 'the Corporation may provide, maintain and equip, (but shall not manufacture), trolley vehicles and may use the same along the whole or any part of the following route, (namely Coventry Road), in the city, 2 miles 7 furlongs and 2.8 chains in length'.

The terminus of the new extension was to be at the city boundary at Tiger's Island, though in the event, because of the lack of a suitable turning point, the actual terminus was at Arden Oak Road, just short of Hatchford Brook, some 0.4 miles inside the city boundary.

The new extension was constructed in the early part of 1936 and was opened on Monday 5 July, with route numbers 94 to Albert Street and 95 to Station Street, although the latter was a peak-hour service that did not operate at all on Sundays. The section from Yardley to Sheldon added 2.51 miles to the existing route along Coventry Road; coupled to the 2.44 miles of the Nechells route, it gave the system its maximum route mileage of 10.18 miles, which would remain for just over four years.

In July 1936 the prototype Leyland six-wheeler, TJ 939, came back to the city, with a new chassis number, an updated chassis specification and a new fleet number of 68. It remained in Birmingham until the end of September 1937, by which time it had run 24,552 miles in revenue service.

Traffic on the Coventry Road services had increased sufficiently, in part because of the Sheldon extension, that further trolleybuses were required to maintain frequencies over the longer distance. In September 1936 12 four-wheeled Leyland TB5 chassis were ordered, with GEC 80hp motors, but this time the updated WT2516J type. The body order went to Metro-Cammell, and the bodies were of a similar style to the contemporary examples being built for BCT on Daimler COG5 chassis. Their seating capacity differed from the buses, being one less at H29/24R, so as to avoid any of the tilt-test problems that had beset the earlier half-cab Leylands. The 12 vehicles were delivered in September 1937 as 67-78 (COX 67-78).

The building of the New Coventry Road at Lyndon End in 1938 was the only major alteration to the system until after the outbreak of the Second World War; the 1935 Act gave the Corporation powers that included discretionary operational powers over existing parts of the route where 'a connecting trolleybus route' became necessary. New Coventry Road was regarded by BCT as part of a one-way-street system despite it being a completely new section of road nearly half a mile long and perhaps not really in the 'spirit' of the 1935 Act!

On the other side of the city, the operating lease on the tram routes beyond the Handsworth boundary and on to West Bromwich, Wednesbury and Dudley was due to expire at the end of 1938. Protracted negotiations took place between West Bromwich Corporation, which was to inherit the operating rights into the Black Country section, and BCT. The former wanted to replace the trams with trolleybuses and proceeded to rebuild Oak Lane garage with sufficient headroom to accommodate the overhead wiring; by late 1937 it appears that they were getting close to actually ordering vehicles. The Dudley and Wednesbury routes would be a joint working with BCT, but the latter acted the role of 'big brother' and refused to entertain the concept of another trolleybus route entering the city. BCT even considered the idea of retaining all the Handsworth tram services within the city boundary, but eventually decided to convert all the 'main-line' tram routes to Dudley with new buses.

On 1 April 1939 the Handsworth, West Bromwich, Wednesbury and Dudley tram routes were abandoned. To operate these services, BCT introduced 85 Leyland 'Titan' TD6cs, while West Bromwich Corporation, the reluctant bus partner, bought 31 new Daimler COG5s.

## Early wartime developments - new vehicles and the suspension of the Nechells route

Ironically, in the same month that the tram services through West Bromwich were abandoned, April 1939, what transpired to be the last Birmingham order for trolleybuses was placed. These were 12 Leyland TB7s, again with GEC WT2516J motors. They were numbered 79-90 (FOK 79-90), and this time the MCCW bodies seated one more, with an H30/24R layout. They entered service between 22 January and 29 February 1940, and for at least one day the operational fleet was 90 vehicles, as on 1 March eight trolleybuses were placed in store.

The Birmingham trolleybus system appeared to be thriving, despite the Corporation's allegiance to the diesel engine, and a system life of at least another 15 years might have been expected, especially as new vehicles had just been delivered.

The Leyland TB7s were nominally replacements for the half-cab Leyland TBD1s, which although only eight years old had all amassed between 140,000 and 201,000 miles. Eight of these 1932-built trolleybuses had been overhauled in 1938. Nos 1, 2 and 3 had not turned a wheel in 1933, and as a result had much lower mileages and were therefore out of synchronisation with the overhaul cycle of the remainder of the class, receiving their overhauls in March 1939, about a year after the rest. Whether the plan was to replace these vehicles when the Leyland TB7s were delivered is not clear. At least five of the half-cabs

had run on peak-hour extras on the Coventry Road route between 1938 and 1940, although never more than two were allocated to that depot at any one time. These trolleybuses can be identified by their monthly mileages on Coventry Road being halved compared to the 2,700 miles a month that they were running on the Nechells route. Yet in 1939 the last three of the COX-registered Leyland TB5s, 73-78, were transferred to Washwood Heath depot to work the Nechells service, suggesting that only some of the older TBD1s were to be pensioned off.

At the end of the service on Leap Year Day 1940, Leyland half-cabs 4-11 were withdrawn and placed in store, probably in the former Sampson Road paintshop, which had recently lost some new FOF-registered Daimler COG5s that had been kept there prior to their entry into service. This left the fleet strength at 82.

From about the time that the West Bromwich negotiations had started in 1937, proposals had been made to abandon the tram system in the city within the next seven years. Although not realised at the time, these discussions were also to have terminal consequences for the small trolleybus system. Various plans were drawn up, but the outbreak of war rather altered the situation. Although the former Company lines beyond the city boundary to Dudley via Smethwick and Oldbury were closed on 30 September 1939, the Ladywood and Lodge Road services, which were due to go at the same time, were reprieved. Similarly, the only other definitely planned route abandonments were the two Stechford tram services, whose 301 Class trams shared depot accommodation at Coventry Road with the trolleybuses; the route was to be closed in April 1940 in advance of the intended widening of Deritend and High Street Bordesley. However, this road-widening scheme was quickly shelved until the end of hostilities, and with it the Stechford tram route closure.

There was no mention of the closure of the somewhat isolated trolleybus routes in the city, and it was anticipated that they would continue intact well beyond the final tramway closure. It would, however, have been interesting to see how the trolleybuses running through Deritend might have been affected had the scheme proceeded.

The first closure came as something as a surprise. As had been the case since 1922, the remaining 14 trolleybuses working on the Nechells service had to gain access to the route overhead by travelling 1½ miles using the power trolleyboom and a trailing skate in the tram rail. Any prospect of putting up negative overhead wires had been lost when the Alum Rock and Washwood Heath trams had been converted to Fischer bow collectors in 1928, as the clearances required for the skate of the bow collector on the tramcar would have fouled the poles of any passing trolleybus.

This problem of gaining access to the trolleybus route at Bloomsbury Street must have been difficult enough in normal circumstances, but in wartime, at night and in the blackout it must have been something of a nightmare! But the real problem lay in the vehicles' method of current collection. Birmingham trolleybuses used trolleywheels; as a result the overhead had to be heavily and regularly greased with graphite to ensure a good current collection. Unfortunately, when used in connection with the trolley-bus skate in the tram rail to act as the electrical return, the dust and grit on the road surface led to a poor contact. This in turn led to a lot of pyrotechnics, which infringed the blackout regulations.

Birmingham's first air raid was on 9 August 1940, when a single German plane bombed the Montague Road area of Erdington. The raids rapidly grew more frequent and heavier, but on Sunday 25 August the first mass night raid took place in the country and it was Birmingham that was targeted. Fifty bombers destroyed the Market Hall in the Bull Ring and the following night a six-hour raid targeted the BSA factory in Small Heath. Because bombing from altitude lacked accuracy, as with all these raids on industrial targets, whole swathes of the city, including residential areas, were destroyed.

Lying on the southern side of the Tame Valley, the Nechells area had in it gas, electric and sewage works, canals, railway marshalling yards, the LMS Aston locomotive depot, as well as many small and large factories that were involved in the production of military matériel. Many of the early air raids were aiming at the nearby Castle Bromwich aircraft factory, and any blackout irregularities were regarded as very serious breaches of the Emergency Powers Acts. The arcing of the Nechells trolleybuses on depot workings in the hours of darkness was an obvious problem, especially as the route ran towards the adjacent part of the Tame Valley that was being targeted by the German Luftwaffe!

Because of the prospect of more air raids, the decision was quickly made in mid-September 1940 to suspend the Nechells trolleybus service until hostilities ended - there was no intention to abandon the route. On Monday 30 September 1940 the trolleybuses ran a normal service throughout the day, then returned to Washwood Heath depot; unannounced, they were replaced by diesel-engined buses on the Tuesday morning. The remaining three Leyland TBD1s, the five AEC 663Ts and 17-21 of the six-wheel Leyland TTBD2s, which were surplus to requirements at Coventry Road after 73-78 returned from their sojourn at Washwood Heath, were taken to the former Sampson Road paintshop and placed in store in two rows against one wall.

Given that the AECs were only seven years old, had fairly low mileages and that there was a natural shortage of trolleybuses in the country, it might have seemed logical to offer them for hire to another operator, such as either Walsall or Wolverhampton Corporation; both municipalities hired 1934-5 vintage Sunbeam MS2s from Bournemouth Corporation during the war period. If, however, the intention was to return the AECs to service in the future, their storage was perhaps understandable. The Corporation appeared to 'fall between two stools', as the trolleybuses, if scrapped, would at least have helped the wartime drive for scrap metal. The five Leyland six-wheelers returned to service in the first week of December 1940; the half-cabs would have been withdrawn anyway, but had the Nechells service been recommenced, the AECs would have been restored to service.

The 7 trolleybus route was replaced by motorbuses, with a route number of 43, to avoid confusion with the 7 bus route to Portland Road. The subsequent decision to close the route appears to have been taken as a result of a slow process of attrition. The 1936 trolleybus blind,

introduced for the Sheldon route extension, had 11 destinations. On the new blinds introduced on 29 October 1941, when the Lode Lane route was opened, adding route numbers 96, 97 and 98, the Nechells route details were omitted. This left 12 destinations listed on the blind. Gradually, after the air raids of November 1940 and April 1941, small sections of trolleybus overhead were cannibalised to provide replacement wiring on damaged sections of tram routes. By 1944 the situation was beyond repeal, with no trolleybuses available, no destination blinds and some of the overhead missing!

## Later wartime developments - the opening of the Lode Lane branch

If the closure of the Nechells route was unique, the next development was similarly unusual. Only two electric traction routes in this country were built under the Emergency Powers Act of 1939, the first using Birmingham trolleybuses and the second, in December 1943, being an extension on the Liverpool tram system of routes 13, 19, 29 and 44A to the Royal Ordnance factory at Kirkby.

In 1938 a site for Rover's new 'Shadow' factory was chosen on agricultural land at the edge of Solihull. Rover was to produce the Bristol 'Hercules' radial aero-engine as part of the Government's plan to concentrate aircraft engine production in Birmingham and Coventry. There was an urgent need for new engines and parts, but there was an equally important requirement to disperse the factories away from the inner parts of the city in order to make them more difficult targets. The factory opened in 1939 and reached full production by September 1940, when the problem of transporting all the factory workers became a considerable headache for Midland Red and a number of independent bus operators. In the summer of 1941 the Ministry of Supply and War Transport provided the authority to build an extension from the Wheatsheaf, along Hobs Moat Road and Lode Lane to the new Rover factory.

Although the site was well outside the Birmingham boundary, it was realised that an extension of the nearby existing electric service was a better option than increasing the bus services run in Solihull UDC by the Birmingham & Midland Motor Omnibus Company (BMMO) as there was a desperate need to conserve fuel oil and petrol at this period of the war.

The new 1½-mile-long extension from Coventry Road was opened on 29 October 1941 into the grounds of the factory by way of a private road. Although initially the route was only worked to coincide with Rover's work shifts, the trolleybuses were allowed to carry passengers other than Rover workers when space permitted. By December 1942 a regular hourly all-day service was being operated. The new routes were numbered 96, from Albert Street, and 97, from Station Street, though the latter was far more frequently used. After the war the Lode Lane service was only run on Mondays to Fridays, except when the demands of the Rover factory required weekend workings.

During the Second World War all the trolleybuses in service were painted with the usual white markings around the edges of the vehicles, masked headlights and khaki roofs. It is thought that two of the Leyland six-wheelers was painted in all-over grey in 1942. Every night between 1941 and 1942 as many as 40 trolleybuses were dispersed and parked, facing the city, in New Coventry Road, between Wagon Lane and Brays Road; this was in case of bomb damage to Coventry Road depot. In 1942 BCT tentatively approached the Ministry of War Transport about the possibility of obtaining extra trolleybuses because of the demands of the new Lode Lane extension to the Rover works. If it had been successful, Birmingham would have operated a batch of Sunbeam W4s with MoWT-style bodies. The response was perhaps not unexpected; the idea was not entertained, as BCT had the 16 Nechells trolleybuses hidden away in store!

By the end of hostilities in Europe in May 1945 it was obvious that the Nechells route would not be re-instated. The stored trolleybuses 1-11, the Leyland TTBD1s and 12-16, the AEC 663Ts, were taken from their 'secret' storage in the former paintshop at Sampson Road, the lease on which was to expire in September 1945. They had shared this accommodation with up to ten bomb- or accident-damaged tramcars for most of the war, and it must be presumed that one of the reasons for both the trolleybus and tram disposals was that the Corporation had received insurance compensation and was therefore bound to dispose of these vehicles for scrap despite the fact that in a number of cases the condition of some of the tramcars was little worse than other trams that were repaired.

The trolleybuses were sold to the nearby scrap dealers Midland Motors of Golden Hillock Road. In 1950 three of the trolleybuses, 1, 8 and 16, were seen in Holland's coach yard in Oldbury. The last of the half-cab Leylands, 11 (OV 4011), was later reputedly seen as a caravan in the Vale of Evesham.

# Decline and fall

After the end of hostilities the fleet was repainted, but without the pre-war gold lining-out on the 17-66 Class. The evening of 15 April 1946 saw the introduction of hourly all-night services on the main roads out of the city. These had their termini either outside Edward Grey's department store in Bull Street or in Colmore Row, beneath the shadow of St Phillip's Cathedral. This obviously precluded the use of trolleybuses on the Coventry Road service, and buses from Acocks Green garage were employed on Coventry Road's night service, the route being numbered NS94A. In reality it was the 93 trolleybus route extended from Station Street into the city by way of Hill Street and the City Centre loop. The suffix 'A' indicated that it did not go to the daytime terminus, as it turned back at the Wagon & Horses Hotel at Lyndon End.

The closure of the 84 and 90 tram routes to Stechford on Saturday 2 October 1948 caused considerable congestion inside Coventry Road depot. About 38 four-wheeled, open-balconied 301 Class tramcars were required in order to operate the two tram routes, and the space occupied by the replacement pre-war Daimler COG5s and the new 1756 Class of Daimler CVD6s was considerably more than that occupied by the trams. As a result not all of the replacement buses could be accommodated in the depot;

an open space at the rear of the premises, with access into Arthur Street, was purchased, and during the next few months a large section of the rear wall of Coventry Road depot was removed in order to gain access to it. In the interim a number of buses operating services run by Coventry Road were accommodated at the nearby Liverpool Street garage until the new door was completed; thereafter the entire bus fleet was able to be garaged at Coventry Road, either under cover with the trolleybuses, or in the new open yard. The trolleybuses still occupied rows 1-6 adjacent to the main entrance as well as rows 16-19 alongside the back wall, although slightly fewer could be parked there because of the new entrance to the Arthur Street yard.

The Lyndon End turn-back, as used by the NS 94A bus service, became the last new section of trolleybus wiring to be opened on 24 January 1949. The ever-increasing traffic demands on the trolleybuses caused by the development of the Sheldon area had begun to cause rush-hour difficulties at Arden Oak Road. The new turn-back was used in the rush hour and was given the route number 99.

The Coventry Road trolleybus service had survived the war reasonably unscathed. It continued to operate an efficient and undisturbed existence in the east of the city and was undoubtedly very successful. However, the system unfortunately had a number of disadvantages. The basic infrastructure dated from 1934, and 50 of the 74 trolleybuses were becoming due for replacement. The real 'nail in the coffin' for the trolleybuses was that they were a tiny proportion of the whole fleet. By 1949 there were still about 415 tramcars available for service, while the bus fleet was in excess of 1,500 vehicles. Although 24 of the trolleybuses were only between nine and 12 years old, the future of the trolleybus service along Coventry Road was in peril.

At the June 1949 meeting of the Transport Committee the proposal to abandon electric traction in the city was adopted. The first tram routes to be abandoned were those to Moseley, Balsall Heath and Kings Heath, in October 1949. Next would be the Perry Barr and Witton service in December; then the Lozells, Washwood Heath and Alum Rock services were to go in October 1950. Then came Stage 4, the abandonment of the Coventry Road trolleybuses at a date set for July 1951!

The Bristol Road and Cotteridge services were to be abandoned in July 1952, while the withdrawal of the three Erdington tram routes in July 1953 would eliminate electric traction in the city. Thus the city's trolleybuses would be survived by about 262 trams, which were between 12 and 21 years older than the newest trolleybuses, while a proportion of the replacement buses drafted into Coventry Road garage would be contemporary to the COX-registered trolleybuses!

Another key factor in the abandonment was that the overhaul facilities at Kyotts Lake Road would be closed down by 1954, after the withdrawal of the tramcars. Although Tyburn Road bus works had been used for trolleybus overhauls and repaints from 1929 until 1933, to use that facility again would have involved a very long tow across the city, which was not really practical for such a insignificant part of the fleet.

The Labour Government's nationalisation of the Electricity Department also meant that the advantages of inter-departmental trading were lost, and the incentive to keep any form of electrical traction operational was dramatically reduced.

The abandonment programme went ahead as planned quite relentlessly. In January 1950 the Corporation applied to the West Midlands Traffic Commissioners for replacement bus licences, and this was quickly granted. The first 30 of the new Daimler CVD6s due for delivery from Metro-Cammell in the summer of 1951 were earmarked as replacement vehicles at Coventry Road garage.

Meanwhile the trolleybus system continued largely undisturbed by its imminent demise. Overhauls continued until March 1950, when six-wheeler 41 (OC 1141) was given the last 'semi-overhaul'. Twelve trolleybuses were given a 'clean and varnish' in a final burst of activity at 'The Lake' in November and December 1950.

The first signs of the closure passed largely unnoticed by the general public. In the recesses of Coventry Road depot, trolleybuses with major electrical and mechanical defects or those with accident damage were quietly laid up. At the end of February 1951 three of the OC-registered trolleybuses, 24, 39 and 51, were withdrawn, and these were followed the next month by 52; in early May 1951 Leyland TB7 88 (FOK 88) was also withdrawn, while in the last month of operation several of the fleet were unofficially 'pensioned off'.

The public notices of the trolleybus conversion scheme were placed at the main bus stops, in the press and in the windows of the trolleybuses in early June 1951. Two 'final' tours of the system were organised, both using BCT's last trolleybus, 90 (FOK 90). The first, by the Omnibus Society, took place on Sunday 3 June, and three weeks later, on 24 June, the Light Railway Transport League did the same.

The trolleybus system closed down during the last two days of June 1951. On Friday 29 June, Leyland TTBD2 45 (OC 1145) left the Rover Works on a 96 service to Albert Street, thus closing the Lode Lane branch, while earlier in the day the last Station Street service was worked.

The following morning, Saturday 30 June, the trolleybuses operated as normal, although by early afternoon redundant vehicles, with fleet numbers and city crests painted out in black, were being towed out of the depot by W. T. Bird's tractor units as part of the first tranche of vehicles to be taken to that company's scrapyard at Stratford-upon-Avon. As this was taking place, an ever-decreasing number of service trolleybuses were continuing to operate the route as normal until about 8.30 pm, when the normal service requirements began to tail off. A farewell party began at Coventry Road depot for all the staff and officials connected with the trolleybuses, which lasted until well after the last trolleybus had returned there.

The final services left Albert Street at just before 11.00 pm, with Leyland TB5 73 (COX 73), followed at 11.02 pm by trolleybus 45 (OC 1145), as the last in public service. The final trolleybus, 90 (FOK 90), was driven by Driver Frederick Gilks (see page 120), and carried the official party from the Transport Committee, leaving the depot at 10.45 pm for the last journey into the city. As it went past Coventry Road depot on its way towards the city boundary, so the first-ever NS 58, an exposed-radiator 1756 Class Daimler CVD6, left the depot to go into the city to take up service at 11.30 pm. After leaving the terminus at Arden Oak Road, the Leyland four-wheel trolleybus returned to Coventry Road garage (as it was now officially known!) just after midnight on 1 July 1951 to close Birmingham's trolleybus system. After 28 years the power was switched off and the trolleybus system, which had begun in a blaze of pioneering publicity, closed with barely a mention in the technical press!

Throughout Sunday 1 July, the remaining trolleybuses were taken away by Bird's. Because of a lack of space at Stratford, some 13 were taken to Cunliffe's yard, in Wellington Road, Handsworth, where they remained for nearly a year before being taken to Stratford.

The Sunday service along Coventry Road was operated by vehicles from the batch of brand-new Daimler CVD6s numbered 2626-2655 (JOJ 626-655). On Monday 2 July the full service of motorbuses commenced, with the new buses being augmented by two-year-old exposed-radiator, HOV-registered Daimler CVD6s. By the end of that day all the complex wiring in front of Coventry Road garage had been taken down, and within two weeks the wiring and the traction poles had been largely removed by the contractors on the rest of the system.

The citizens of Small Heath, Yardley and Sheldon were none too pleased at the loss of their excellent 'Silent Service'. The new buses provided fewer stops per mile and a less frequent service; they were slower, noisier and had a lower seating capacity!

The Birmingham trolleybus system had the dubious distinction of being outlived by the trams that at one time it seemed destined to replace! Today virtually nothing is left to suggest that trolleybuses ever ran in the city, either on the Nechells or the Coventry Road routes. The most tangible surviving feature is the old turning circle at Hay Mills, but even this is fenced off!

Only one vehicle survives, albeit as a petrol-engined bus; this is the very first Leyland TBD1 trolleybus, OV 1175, which is now beautifully restored as MJX 222J in Halifax livery. Even this survivor, which was one of the few demonstrators to operate in the city not to be painted in BCT's distinguished blue and cream livery, has little to show that it was ever part of Birmingham's trolleybus fleet!

# THE NECHELLS ROUTE

THE FIRST TRAM SERVICE to Nechells was opened by the City of Birmingham Tramways Company on 11 November 1884, starting from Albert Street at a point near the Park Street junction. It survived until 31 December 1906, being the last horse tram route in the city. Birmingham Corporation took over the operation on Tuesday 1 January 1907 with electric trams, which ran from its city terminus in Martineau Street. At the end of the First World War the track was in a very poor state, and after much deliberation the decision was made to convert the route to trolleybus operation.

The Nechells trolleybus 7 route was opened on 27 November 1922 and replaced the tram route of the same number. The trolleybus terminus was in Old Square, some 400 yards further out of the city centre along Corporation Street from the former tram terminus. Old Square was very elegantly laid out in 1697 and completed with Queen Anne-style buildings. The original houses were demolished when Corporation Street was cut through to Aston Road in the late 1880s.

## A ride along the route

The Nechells trolleybus route had its terminus in a loop beneath the brooding presence of the former Newbury's department store. The loading stop was situated immediately before the buses turned left into Corporation Street and joined the Perry Barr tram route. The overhead wiring along the Nechells route was set at 13 inches separation using tramway-type arched hangers; no frogs were employed, although shared tramway junctions often posed a problem. For a short distance the Alum Rock and Washwood Heath trams also went along Corporation Street. The James Watt Street junction caused operational problems for the trolleybuses after the Washwood Heath depot's tram services were converted to bow-collectors. Inbound trolleybuses, operating up the hill passing the Victoria Law Courts, had to coast over the overhead in order to gain their route to Old Square, which made life very difficult for the trolleybus motormen. Any tram equipped with poles coming out of the city and turning right had also to coast over the overhead frog with its pole down, otherwise it would foul the trolleybus overhead.

On their way out from the central shopping area, the trolleybuses descended Corporation Street and were met by the Erdington group of trams coming out of Steelhouse Lane by the General Hospital. The trolleybuses crossed Corporation Place, then went along Aston Street as far as Gosta Green. Here they forked right in front of the Sacks of Potatoes into Lister Street and over the humped-back bridge crossing the Birmingham & Fazeley Canal before travelling out towards the distant gas works at Nechells and Saltley along Great Lister Street. This area was a mixture of mid-19th century terraced houses, shops

and small workshops, which extended towards the Rea Valley in Saltley, some half a mile away.

Just before Saltley Road the normal service trolleybuses turned left into Bloomsbury Street, along which there was the usual two sets of overhead wiring, but around the corner into Saltley Road there extended two single sets of wires, unconnected to the service car's wires.

These were used as feeders for the nearby Washwood Heath tramcars (see the inset in the map overleaf). On journeys to and from Washwood Heath depot, about 1½ miles away, the trolleybuses employed the positive tram overhead and a chain 'skate' dragged along in the groove fitted into the tram track to return the current. They went along Washwood Heath Road to 'The Gate' at Saltley, over Saltley Viaduct and into Saltley Road to the Great Francis Street junction. In the shadow of the former London & North Western Railway bridge, the trolleybuses were then put on to the 300-yard section of single tram overhead wiring in Saltley Road and were driven inwards towards the city until the Bloomsbury Street junction was reached. Just before the overhead feeder near the junction, the wires forked into two single power lines; these took the trolleybuses either around the corner into Bloomsbury Street or into Great Lister Street. At each of these points the trolleybuses were transferred to the appropriate set of service wires. This tedious process was done in reverse for trolleybuses returning to their depot; this happened to every trolleybus working on the Nechells service, day and night, for 18 years!

The premises at the junction of Great Lister Street and Bloomsbury Street were a little older than those nearer the city, dating from immediately before the rapid industrial expansion that swept away the nearby Vauxhall Gardens in 1850, which had been one of the sights of Regency Birmingham. These houses were built at the edge of the Ashted Estate development, a 'first generation' suburb of Birmingham.

At Bloomsbury Street the trolleybuses joined the route of the former horse-tram service and climbed in a north-easterly direction towards Nechells Green. This was the only turn-back point on the route, put into position about 1928, and was shown on the destination blinds as NECHELLS GREEN ONLY. There was a loop here, but it was without frogs, which meant that the facility to turn round was of little practical advantage! Only the skill of the trolleybus drivers and a slight slope enabled this manoeuvre to be undertaken, though in reality it was rarely done.

Nechells Green, at the corner of Nechells Place, sounds idyllic, but it was a shopping area made up of converted Victorian terraced houses; it was also known as High Park Corner. The trolleybuses did not use the former outward route of the trams via Thimblemill Lane and Long Acre, but substituted two-way working along Nechells Park Road. Here the shops gave way to houses as the former horse tram depot in Butlin Street was passed on the way

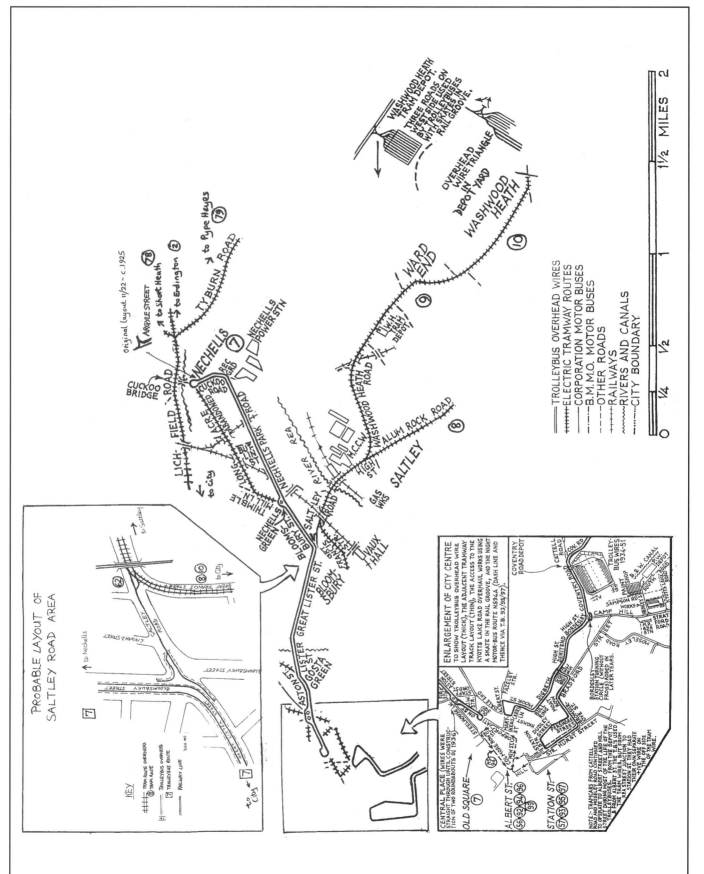

The Nechells trolleybus route, with an enlargement of the city centre and an inset showing the probable layout of the overhead in Saltley Road.

to the junction with Holborn Hill. Clustered around this crossroads were some more shops, a large public house and the decoratively styled Nechells Public Baths.

Beyond Holborn Hill, Nechells Park Road descended a tree-lined hill. Near the top of the hill were some slightly superior bay-windowed terraced houses with wrought-iron-topped front garden walls. At the bottom of the hill, at the Nechells Park Hotel, the trolleybuses turned left and travelled along Cuckoo Road, parallel to the Tame Valley, before reaching the terminus at the junction with Long Acre. The terminus was just short of the Birmingham & Fazeley Canal, and within 200 yards of the Erdington group of tram routes that travelled along Lichfield Road. Until about 1925 the trolleybuses used a reverser into Argyle Street, but this was replaced by a turning circle at the intersection of Cuckoo Road with Long Acre (see map).

The 2½-mile journey had gone from the bustling city centre at Old Square to this depressing area. The terraced houses were surrounded by factories and workshops; less than half a mile away were the all-pervasive odours from Nechells Power Station.

## Vehicle types used on Nechells route

The Nechells route was the only one in the city to operate all three generations of Birmingham's trolleybuses; the original 'trackless' fleet of mainly Railesses ran from 1922 until 1932, while from 1930 to 1933 five demonstrators were tested on the route. The second-generation trolleybuses were the Leyland TBD1 half-cabs that replaced the Railless fleet; these were quickly joined by the six-wheeled AEC 663Ts of 1932, and both classes operated on the Nechells service until 1940. In this last year of operation, the final six vehicles from the modern-looking COX-registered batch of Leyland TB5s worked the service, augmenting the three surviving TBD1s and the five AECs until the suspension of the trolleybus service.

**The Old Square was redeveloped from a lovely, genteel early-18th-century square into a three-sided open space. It was an extension of the bustling Corporation Street, which formed the southern side of the square. In the background is the New Theatre, opened on 14 November 1883 and immediately renamed the Grand Theatre, despite retaining its original name on the entablature!**

**The operation of steam trams from Old Square began in November 1884 with a route to Perry Barr operated by Birmingham Central Tramways (BCT), whose offices were contained in a Queen Anne town house in the square on the corner with Upper Priory.**

**The City of Birmingham Tramways Co Ltd was incorporated to acquire the business and assets of the former BCT on 29 September 1896, and it is one of their Beyer Peacock steam locomotives, 61 of 1886, and the last of 20 Falcon-built trailers, also of 1886, number 74, a 60-seater with stairs at each end, that are standing on the exit part of the track loop around the square. It is about the turn of the century and the steam trams would last until the last day of 1906. Old Square would remain free of trams from that time, but public transport would return on 27 November 1922 with the 'new-fangled tracklesses'.** *J. Whybrow collection*

**Standing at a set of points in Bartholomew Street, near the Albert Street terminus, is a Nechells horse tram owned by the City of Birmingham Tramways Company. This service was begun on 11 November 1884 and was operated by BCT; it left Albert Street by way of Curzon Street and Bloomsbury Street to Nechells, where, in Butlin Street, there was the stables and car depot.**

**In order to get the tramcars up the hill into Albert Street a trace horse was used, conveniently identifiable in this case as the white one. The service was lettered 'F' and survived until 31 December 1906. On New Year's Day 1907 Birmingham Corporation began its replacement electric tram service from Martineau Street.** *Dudley Library*

**Above** The first trolleybuses to be delivered to Birmingham were 12 Railless F12 vehicles fitted with Charles Roe H25/26RO bodies. Not only were these the first double-deckers to be bodied by Roe, but they were also the first batch of top-covered trolleybuses in the country. They were 16 ft 3½ in high and used the standard Schiemann system of current collection with trolleypoles strung beneath the wires with the contact being made through a trolley wheel.

No 11 (OK 4833) stands in the Old Square with its top deck fully laden and the lower saloon empty. This photograph was taken about 1924, before these vehicles received their first repaint, and shows the original style of the livery with cream rocker panels and, unusually, the City of Birmingham crest mounted on the cream since the blue-painted panel above was too narrow. *R. Marshall*

**Below** An AEC 602 demonstrator, fitted with a B36R body and painted in a red and white livery, came to Birmingham on a sale or return basis. It was registered OL 994 and was tried out on the newly opened Nechells route from 17 August 1923 until late October the same year, during which short time it ran some 4,342 miles. Unlike later demonstrators it was not given a fleet number. With its somewhat tram-like single-deck body, OL 994 is seen at the city terminus in the Old Square. *R. Marshall*

Railless 11 (OK 4833) is seen again at the Old Square terminus in about 1931 and by now is carrying a slightly modified livery, which was introduced when the trolleybuses were transferred to Tyburn Road bus works for overhauling and repainting. The area below the lower saloon windows is painted blue while the canopy over the cab is painted cream. This trolleybus was to remain in service until February 1932.

Similar Railless vehicles were delivered to Nottingham in 1926, but these were converted to pneumatic tyres, which gave them both a more modern appearance as well as improving the ride for the passengers. The BCT Raillesses ran all their ten-year lives on solid tyres, averaging some 230,000 miles each. This was something of a triumph as they rattled over the cobbled streets shuttling to and from Nechells. *C. F. Klapper*

The production of the early trackless trolleybuses had been mainly confined to specialist constructors until the mid-1920s when a number of motorbus manufacturers began to dabble in the new mode of transport. Birmingham bought one AEC, 17 (ON 3261), which was the only 607-type model to be constructed. This former demonstrator had a H26/26RO body by Vickers, who, rather like the more successful Short Brothers, briefly built bus bodies from the mid-1920s until 1929. After that year the company reverted to aircraft manufacturing, and as far as is known this was the only trolleybus body that they built.

No 17, which had the distinction of being the first trolleybus on the system to be fitted with a foot-controller, was the last of Birmingham's solid-tyred 'trackless' vehicles. It entered service on 3 March 1926 and had a service life of only six years, during which time ran some 99,585 miles. It is parked in the Old Square in August 1929 outside Crane's piano shop, which stood on the corner of the square and Corporation Street. *G. H. F. Atkins*

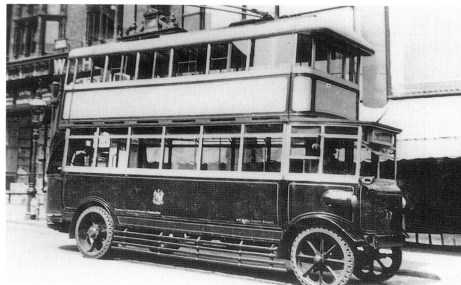

The second generation of trolleybuses that replaced the 'trackless' fleet were the equally unusual half-cab Leyland TBD1s, which were equipped with GEC 65hp motors and Short Brothers 48-seater bodies. No 8 (OV 4015) was one of two members of the class of 11 vehicles that were originally registered and numbered out of sequence, until it could acquire its correct number within the batch. It is seen in the Old Square on 19 July 1938 and has been re-fitted with roller-blind destination equipment and the brass-rimmed headlights that had been taken off in 1932 as a weight-saving measure when the first member of the class failed the tilt-test and had to be reduced in weight. *J. Cull*

*Top* Parked at the Old Square terminus, with its nearside cab door open, also on 19 July 1938, is 16 (OJ 1016), the last of the AEC 663Ts fitted with Brush H33/25R bodies. These were the first six-wheeled trolleybuses in the fleet, and for the first time a Birmingham trolleybus actually looked like a sleek, modern vehicle! In the early 1930s designers of trolleybus bodies tended to produce vehicles with bulbous front aprons below the windscreen, often the vestiges of the shape of a radiator. The front of this new body introduced a straight profile that replaced the 'piano-front' design found on the Leyland TBD1s of the previous year. The Brush Company had supplied Birmingham with tram and bus bodies since 1920, but these would be the last batch of bodies built at Loughborough for BCT until 1943.

This trolleybus was the end product of a long saga of rebuilding and rebodying. It was built in 1930 as the second AEC 663T and was fitted with an English Electric five-bay body. This proved to be unsatisfactory and was scrapped, while the chassis was rebuilt as 663T070 to become the last of BCT's 12-16 Class. *J. Cull*

*Middle* The first of the AEC 663Ts with Brush 58-seater bodies was 12 (OJ 1012). Although largely in as-delivered condition, the original front destination box aperture has been reduced in size to accommodate the standard 34-inch-wide destination blinds. It is waiting in the Old Square at the loading stop in about 1936, in company with some parked delivery vans and cars. These impressive-looking trolleybuses had disappointingly short lives as they were withdrawn at the end of September 1940 when the 'temporary closure' of the Nechells trolleybus route took place. It does seem a great pity that, only eight years old, they were not re-employed on the Coventry Road route or offered for sale or hire to other operators.

In the background, beyond the Armstrong-Siddeley Twelve-Six car, can just be seen the Gaumont cinema in Steelhouse Lane, which opened on 19 February 1931 with a gala performance of *Raffles* starring Ronald Coleman. *R. Wilson*

*Bottom* Being manhandled around the Old Square in front of the framework of Lewis's department store extension is one of the Leyland TTBD2 six-wheeled trolleybuses. It is in grey primer and has no distinguishing markings, although an oval sign in a lower saloon side window proudly proclaims that it has an MCCW metal-framed body. The trolleybus carries the trade-plate 098 VP, and although unregistered it is almost certainly 17 (OC 1117), as this vehicle did not enter service with the Corporation until 25 March 1934, some two months after almost all of the rest of the class. Why it was necessary to push the trolleybus around the top of Old Square when the loop was wired up anyway is uncertain, but there is a policeman in attendance. Despite all this effort, there is no evidence that any of these 17-66 Class ever ran in service on the Nechells route. Birmingham Post

*Top* On a rainy day in March 1932 the driver of Leyland TBD1 9 (OV 4009) prepares to get into the cab before starting out on the 2-mile 772-yard service to Nechells. In the background is Lewis's, the first department store in Birmingham. By this time Lewis's, which had opened its own large retail premises in 1887, had taken over Newbury's premises, which was demolished in 1932 and replaced by the fine example of art deco architecture that was used by Lewis's until it closed on 13 July 1991. It has since been re-developed as offices and small retail units.

The half-cab trolleybus, with its dummy radiator, shows only a paper sticker with the uncompromising NECHELLS in the destination aperture; the original winding gear and box were removed following the tilt-test failure. After about 1937, with relaxed unladen weight limits, the original seating capacity was restored and the destination boxes replaced, and these unusual trolleybuses were able once again to display the full blind display **NECHELLS 7.** *D. R. Harvey collection*

*Middle* The last three of the 67-78 Class of Leyland TB5 trolleybuses were transferred to Washwood Heath depot from Coventry Road in September 1939 and stayed there until the service was curtailed one year later. Photographs of these vehicles working on the Nechells route are therefore extremely rare. Trolleybus 78 (COX 78) is in the Old Square just before leaving the terminus and turning left into Corporation Street. It is equipped with headlight masks, a camouflaged roof and white blackout edgings. In front of the trolleybus are the tracks of the Witton, Perry Barr and Washwood Heath tram routes that had their city terminus in Martineau Street. *R. Wilson*

*Bottom* By 1996 the Old Square is barely recognisable. The corner of the former Lewis's store is on the extreme left and is the only building to have survived from the 1940 photograph. The buildings behind 2314 (KJW 314W), a 1981 MCW 'Metrobus' Mk I, replaced the older premises, which included the locally well-known Crane's piano store, in the 1970s. In 1996, on the other side of Old Square, a statue was erected to the memory of the late Tony Hancock, who was born in Hall Green. The statue is opposite the block that 2314 is passing, which houses the premises of the National Blood Transfusion Service. The perfect irony! *D. R. Harvey*

*Above* The old Newbury's store sits gloomily at the north end of the Old Square in March 1932, not long before it was demolished. A woman with a fox-fur around her neck is about to board Leyland TBD1 2 (OV 4002), one of the GEC 65hp vehicles that had only recently replaced the original fleet of Raillesses.

These Leyland vehicles were ordered as a result of Birmingham courting the Witton-based GEC company to fit a traction motor to a bus chassis. Leyland was approached and the demonstrator, a converted TD1 vehicle, OV 1175, was successfully tested on the Nechells route. Leyland Motors, seeing the trolleybus market being eaten up by AEC, put the design into production, and appropriately the first order was placed by Birmingham Corporation. *Leyland Motors*

*Below* Leyland Motors monitored the progress of the Birmingham TBD1 trolleybuses, as they were the first production batch of four-wheelers that the company had manufactured. They produced a sequence of official publicity photographs, but unfortunately only concentrated their efforts at the more photogenic Old Square end of the route.

Almost new, but slightly mud-splattered, 10 (OV 4010) negotiates its way through a group of pedestrians as it turns out of Old Square into Corporation Street. It has passed the parked, locally built Morris-Commercial canvas-tilt lorry. Just visible above the trolleybus's lower saloon ventilators is the bamboo pole used to rewire the trolley-booms. Behind the white-coated policeman is the Minories, infamous in later years as the site of suicide attempts from the roof of Lewis's store. *Ribble Enthusiasts Club*

*Top* Almost new Leyland TBD1 15 (OV 4015) stands in the Old Square next to the impressive roller-blind stop sign displaying CARS LOAD HERE FOR NECHELLS. Neither the newspaper-seller nor the trolleybus appears to be doing much business!

This vehicle was one of two of the Short-bodied half-cab trolleybuses that were originally given out-of-sequence registration and fleet numbers, the other being 4 (OV 4013). This was because the Railless vehicles that they were intended to replace were retained in service until 31 August 1932. The rather dated piano-front design of these 11 trolleybuses belied their more modern appearance from the rear. To comply with the 1930 Road Traffic Act regulations, an 18-inch rear platform cut-away was included in the design, as was the opening upper saloon emergency exit. *R. Wilson*

*Middle* Railless trolleybus 11 (OK 4833) is about to turn from Corporation Street into Old Square on 14 May 1931, waiting for the man to complete his dash across the busy street and for the 1930-registered Austin Seven to pass in the opposite direction. Roe-bodied 51-seater trolleybus 11 had only eight months left in service, eventually amassing a total of 229,471 miles. By 1931 the contemporary AEC 504 and 507 outside-staircase double-deckers had all been put on pneumatic tyres, leaving these Raillesses as the last solid-tyred vehicles in the Birmingham fleet. Following the trolleybus is a Vulcan-bodied AEC 'Regent' of 1930, with a body style that would echo the replacement trolleybuses of 1932. *D. R. Harvey collection*

*Bottom* Birmingham's first trolleybus, 1 (OK 4823), crests the rise of Corporation Street on its way to the terminus in Old Square. It has just passed Mitchells & Butlers' Marshall Foch public house, which retained the name of the French First World War Allied Commander until the mid-1930s, and is about to cross the outbound tramlines of the Washwood Heath routes at the junction with James Watt Street. When the 8 and 10 routes were converted to bow-collectors in 1928, this junction caused a good deal of difficulty as the trolleybuses had to coast uphill over it. This view was taken after September 1928, as the trolleybus negative wire has been fitted with a long 'dead' section and the bow-collector overhead for the 762-811 Class tramcars has been further protected by the addition of extra wiring to ensure that the bow took the curve. As the trolleybus still retains the old style of blue-painted canopy over the driver's cab and did not receive its last repaint until December 1928, this dates this photograph to within three months.

The Raillesses, though almost as tall and equally as gaunt-looking as the contemporary Birmingham tramcars, had a less ungainly look when on the move. No 1 is, however, still dwarfed by the buildings in Corporation Street such as the distant tower of the Methodist Central Hall, designed by Ewan and James Harder and opened in 1903. *R. Wilson*

*Top* The policeman on point duty wearing a white summer coat in Corporation Street at the junction with John Watt Street is hardly overworked as Railless 3 (OK 4825) comes into town on another journey from Nechells. It is being followed by an early Austin Seven and a bull-nosed Morris Oxford, which are also on their way into the city centre.

It is 1927 and the trolleybus is still in its original-style livery. The tram on the 6 service going in the opposite direction is one of the original 1-20 Class trams that by this date had been rebuilt with enclosed platforms. *P. Boehm, Dusseldorf; D. F. Potter collection*

*Middle* The Victoria Law Courts were completed in 1890 and represented the last stage of Victorian civic development in Birmingham. This had started with the building of the Town Hall in 1834 and reached its peak in 1874 with construction of the Council House. The following year, when the Artisans Dwelling Act enabled slum property to be swept away, Joseph Chamberlain grasped the chance to clear a space and create 'a great street, as broad as a Parisian boulevard'. This became Corporation Street.

The first of the Leylands, 1 (OV 4001), accelerates past the Law Courts and the James Watt Street junction in Corporation Street. When the order for these 11 trolleybuses was placed, in an attempt to support local industry in the Depression the body contract was awarded to John Buckingham, whose factory was in Deritend. In addition, the company was contracted to build the last five bodies on the 1931 order for 20 AEC 'Regent' chassis. Unfortunately the orders came too late to save Buckingham's from becoming another victim of the economic crash, and they went into receivership. The five AECs were given all-metal bodies by Metro-Cammell as part of the 484-503 Class, while the trolleybus order went to Short Brothers, which was building similar-looking but composite-construction bodies on the previous batch of AECs. *G. H. F. Atkins*

*Bottom* The splendid terracotta frontage has not changed since the days of the Nechells trolleys. MCW 'Metrobus' Mk I 2379 (LOA 379X) leaves the city on a 65 service to Short Heath in June 1996. Back in 1932 Corporation Street was a main route out of the city centre, but since the 1980s the road has been truncated and now only buses can gain access on to the Queensway. The Central Fire Station, in the distance, replaced older buildings about a year after Geoff Atkins took the previous photograph, and was opened by HRH The Duke of Kent on Monday 2 December 1935. *D. R. Harvey*

**Top** Short-bodied Leyland TBD1 11 (OV 4011) is about to enter Corporation Place, then on to the lower part of Corporation Street on its way to Gosta Green. It is March 1932 and the trolleybus has only been in service for a few weeks.

There are two Corporation employees washing the impressive street light to the right of the trolleybus, while there is also a window cleaner polishing the first-floor Dutch-styled bay windows of the Edwardian-built shops on the left.

Following the trolleybus is ER&TCW-bodied tram 5, one of the original 1-20 Class delivered in 1904; it is operating on the 6 route to Perry Barr. This tram was one of ten of the class that were destroyed in an air raid on the night of 9-10 April 1941 when an oil bomb was dropped on Miller Street depot. *Leyland Motors*

**Middle** All the buildings at the bottom end of Corporation Street below the Methodist Central Hall, on which the window cleaner was working, were demolished when the nearby Inner Ring Road was being built.

This part of Corporation Street had not been completed until the turn of the century, and prospective developers began to get 'cold feet' after the initial euphoria of the original Corporation Street development scheme. The hard-headed businessmen of the late 19th century were correct in assessing that the profit-making retail area between New Street and the Old Square could not be justifiably extended towards Corporation Place, and for many years this part of the 'Parisian boulevard' was very run-down.

Today the partly truncated Corporation Street has seen something of a revival. Fortunately, most of the Victorian buildings were retained and the 'pull it down and replace it' philosophy of the 1960s has been replaced by a much more enlightened view of Birmingham's heritage. But the trolleybuses have gone! *D. R. Harvey*

**Bottom** After the rebuilding of Corporation Place, which started in 1933, the trams, irrespective of their route, passed through the centre of the newly installed island. Car 668, a Brush-bodied totally enclosed EMB Burnley bogie tram of 1925, leaves the city centre on the 79 service to Pype Hayes.

In this September 1937 view AEC 663T trolleybus 12 (OJ 1012) is negotiating the traffic island on its way into the city from Nechells and the nearby Gosta Green. It has just crossed the tram tracks, which went into Stafford Street then on to the city terminus in Martineau Street. *D. R. Harvey collection*

Passing through Gosta Green on a trial run in September 1932 is brand new AEC 663T trolleybus 15 (OJ 1015). In the background is the Sacks of Potatoes public house, and behind the trolleybus is the mock-Egyptian frontage of the Delicia cinema, opened on Bonfire Night 1923 and finally closed in 1946; it later became the BBC television studio in Birmingham.

Although only seven months separated the AECs from the half-cab Leylands of the 1-11 Class, these five vehicles were much more elegant trolleybuses. They foreshadowed many of the styling features of both the 17-66 Class of Leyland TTBD2s of 1934 and the first batches of Daimler COG5 motorbuses. In the background is a Brush-built tram of 1921, working on the 2 route to Erdington. *D. R. Harvey collection*

Very little of the old Gosta Green remains today, though the Sacks of Potatoes remains as a watering-hole for students of the University of Aston. The old Delicia cinema, hidden behind the trees, is now Dillons University bookshop. Behind the signpost is the line of Corporation Street. As for the rest of Gosta Green, it is now a pedestrianised area within the university campus. *D. R. Harvey*

Despite its poor quality this photograph, taken from a movie film, is included because it is the only known photograph of a trolleybus on this part of the Nechells route. Guy-bodied BTX demonstrator 18 (UK 8341) is on its way into the city and is climbing the hill leading to the Birmingham & Fazeley Canal bridge in Lister Street near the old Holt No 2 brewery, having crossed the Dartmouth Street junction at the bottom of the hill. The trolleybus was demonstrated to Birmingham Tramways & Omnibus Department from 22 February 1930 until the end of May 1931, but no orders were forthcoming from the undertaking. *Guy Motors*

*Below* The Railless trolleybuses, with their hand-controllers, must have required a lot of driving skill. With their solid tyres and narrow tram-style bodies they weighed 7 tons 6 cwt unladen; although only half the weight of a bogie tramcar, they must have been a trial of strength for the drivers, especially when carrying their full complement of 51 passengers. The conductor of trolleybus 5 (OK 4827) poses on a rainy day about 1924 on the recently abandoned tram tracks in Great Lister Street. *D. R. Harvey collection*

*Above* Once beyond Gosta Green, the trolleybuses went along Great Lister Street as far as the junction with Saltley Road, where Roe-bodied Railless 5 (OK 4827) is seen turning into Bloomsbury Street. Behind the road repairs is the Turk's Head public house, Wallis's shop spills its groceries on to the street, and a carter unloads his horse-drawn dray. The four sets of wire can be seen, but the one on the right, used for the depot workings, was not connected to either of the route wires and trolleybuses had to be re-poled here before and after entering revenue service (see the map on page 16). After turning into Bloomsbury Street, the route climbed to Nechells Green, passing through an area of Victorian houses towards the Great Francis Street junction. *C. Carter*

*Below* This area was totally swept away in the early 1950s comprehensive redevelopment of Nechells, part of one of the five Central Development Area rebuilding plans; only the nearby library and the odd public house was left standing, although the Turk's Head pub, which stood roughly where the road sign is on the extreme right, has long since gone. Replaced by multi-storey flats and maisonette blocks, they in turn have been demolished after a life of barely 35 years. The tower block at Nechells Green at the top of Bloomsbury Street is the sole survivor from the mass demolition of recent years. The rest of the buildings in this view are the replacement 'town houses' that were erected in the late 1980s.

The distant West Midlands Buses' Leyland 'Lynx' single-decker is working on the 66A route, which follows in part the trolleybus replacement 43 service to the same Nechells terminus at Cuckoo Road. *D. R. Harvey*

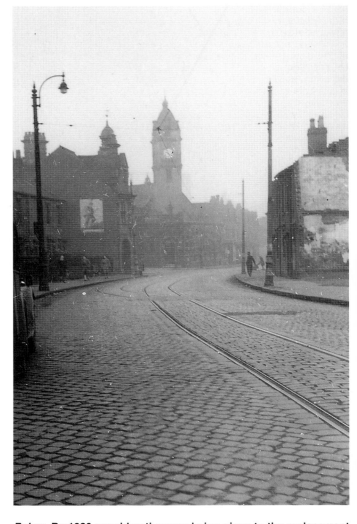

*Above* Another view of the junction as Railless F12 trolleybus 9 (OK 4831) turns into Bloomsbury Street after negotiating the same roadworks. To the left is the pair of overhead wires leading from Bloomsbury Street, at the Turk's Head pub, into Saltley Road; these were used for workings to Washwood Heath depot, but only extended as far as the tram overhead at Great Francis Street. Beyond that point a skate in the tram tracks was used. Just visible above the chimney of the tar-boiler are the sets of hangers for the trolleybuses going towards the city. *D. R. Harvey collection*

*Right* The clock tower of the Bloomsbury Free Library, on the corner of Lingard Street, emerges from the gloom as a woman pushing a handcart starts to cross Saltley Road. Opposite it is the smaller tower of the local Fire Station. The track and the single power overhead line in Saltley Road were kept in place after the closure of the Nechells tram route in November 1922; the latter was used by trolleybuses travelling between Washwood Heath depot and the Bloomsbury Street junction where a trailing skate in the tramlines was used, as this section of the route was never wired for trolleybuses.

After the route was suspended in 1940, the track and the overhead remained in position until after the Washwood Heath route closures in October 1950. The nearest power feeder, near the corner of Bloomsbury Street, had to remain in position as it was part of the Washwood Heath tram's power supply and not, surprisingly, attached to the trolleybus supply; this is why it survived for ten years after the trolleybus route suspension! The disconnected track loop between the nearer traction poles is a remnant of the short-lived Martineau Street to Saltley via Great Lister Street service, which began on 7 August and closed on 11 September 1907. This was the only time that service tramcars ever ran on this part of Saltley Road. *J. S. Webb*

*Below* By 1930 consideration was being given to the replacement of the solid-tyred Railless fleet and a number of demonstrators were tried out, including two virtually identical vehicles hired from Guy Motors. Guys built three demonstrators in 1930: the one seen here, UK 8341, its 'twin' OG 9886 and a previously unregistered demonstrator that eventually became TH 5167. The first two came to Birmingham, while all three found their way into the Llanelly & District fleet in 1935, with UK 8341 being re-registered TH 5166.

Perversely, 18 (UK 8341), registered in Wolverhampton, was to stay with Birmingham Corporation for 17 months, while the Birmingham-registered 19 (OG 9886) only stayed for the week of 10-17 April 1931. No 18 is seen at High Park Corner at the junction with Thimble Mill Road in February 1930, undertaking clearance trials on the Nechells route a few days after being received. It was fitted with a Rees-Turbo 60hp motor and, despite its size, only seated 53 passengers. A contemporary Wolverhampton Corporation Guy-bodied Guy BTX, 78 (UK 9978), survives, somewhat remarkably, at the Black Country Museum in Dudley. *Courtesy of Travel West Midlands*

As the pedestrians scurry along in the rain, Railless F13-type trolleybus 8 (OK 4830) avoids the road works in Nechells Park Road made necessary by the lifting of the tram tracks, the removal of which on the Nechells route was apparently done in a somewhat piecemeal fashion; it is near the maximum extent of its trolley-poles as it manoeuvres past the obstruction. Only the three-storied building beyond the pedestrians on the left remains today from this 1923 scene looking towards the city. The rise in the road behind the trolleybus is the railway bridge over the former LNWR line to Perry Barr.

The introduction of the term 'trolley omnibuses' can be attributed to Alfred Baker, the General Manager, who in a paper in *Tramway and Railway World* of 20 September 1923 stated that he disapproved of the expression 'railless', which had been in common usage until that time. *Ribble Enthusiasts Club*

Taken from the top deck of a trolleybus within a few months of the opening of the route, Nechells Park Road was a typical late-Victorian development that still had the luxury of trees alongside the main road. Unfortunately there are no trolleybuses in this view, looking towards Holborn Hill crossroads. The single-line tram tracks have yet to be removed and the trolleybus wiring is held on the single-arm brackets offset to the out-of-city direction.

The section from Bloomsbury Street to the terminus was also used for trolleybus driver training. During October and November 1922 the first five of the 1-12 Class ran quite substantial mileages prior to the route opening, this section of the Nechells tram route being closed down to allow this to take place. Passengers going from Bloomsbury Street to the terminus used a temporary motorbus service.

The corner shop of J. Morse is not only a grocer but also a wine merchant, further adding to the impression that this was still a reasonably 'middle class' area. On the opposite side of the road is the Methodist church, and beyond that a small row of shops that occupied the frontage of Nechells Park Road as far as Trevor Street. *D. F. Potter collection*

The Victorian houses in Nechells Park Road were mainly demolished in the 1960s and for many years the road ran through derelict land. Redevelopment finally came in the 1980s and has made the scene nearly unrecognisable.

On the skyline, at the junction with Holborn Hill, is the tower of Nechells Baths. This splendidly indulgent piece of municipal Victorian architecture, which is on the right through the trees in the 1923 view, is unfortunately closed and under threat of demolition. Not only has the large Methodist church in the earlier photograph been replaced by a modern, more anonymous building, but Morse's shop, as well as all the other shops, and Stella Street have disappeared! It would be nice to think that the tall tree on the right was the same as that on the extreme right in 1923. *D. R. Harvey*

*Top* Guy BTX 18 (UK 8341) was filmed for Guy Motors in February 1930 when it was demonstrated on the Nechells route, and parts of the route thus recorded were never photographed again. Painted in full BCT livery, 18 is descending Nechells Park Road having crested the distant rise at the Holborn Hill junction. The photograph also shows that the area, with its terraced housing and small walled front gardens, was a distinct step up the social ladder from nearby Duddeston, Vauxhall or the inner parts of Aston. *Guy Motors*

*Middle* The only remnants from 1930 to have survived today are the sections of wall on the left-hand side of Nechells Park Road at the corner of Needham Street. The area was in need of housing redevelopment 30 years after the Guy trolleybus was filmed, and this was done in the 1970s and early 1980s, removing, of course, many of the old streets and courtyards.

This part of Nechells has always been something of a backwater. Nechells Park Road has today returned to being a minor road between more important routeways including the M6, the Aston Expressway and the Heartlands Development Spine Road. The old shopping centre has disappeared and as a result the area is far quieter than it was 70-odd years ago. *D. R. Harvey*

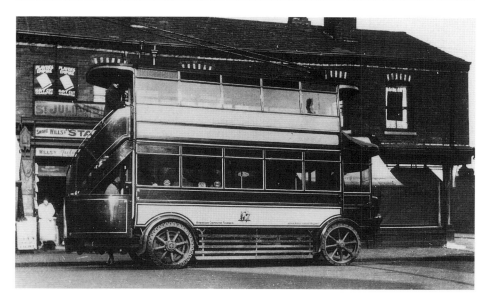

*Left* The corner shops that sold everything were given the somewhat derogatory name of 'hucksters', but were best portrayed in the excellent BBC comedy series *Open All Hours*. Behind the unidentified Railless F13 trolleybus of the 1-12 Class, which is parked in Cuckoo Road, is such a shop, contained in a terrace of 1860s-built houses. Judging by the advertisements on its frontage it seems to be only selling tobacco products, with adverts for Player's Navy Cut cigarettes, two brands of Wills's cigarettes and St Julian tobacco.

An intending passenger has climbed the outside staircase and is about to enter the top-covered upper saloon. Perhaps he is going to smoke one of the cigarettes that he might have just bought from the shop. These enclosed double-deckers were real 'trail-blazers' and briefly put the Corporation at the forefront of trolleybus development in this country. Except for

*Top* Leyland TBD1 2 (OV 4002) has left the terminus at Cuckoo Road and passes the Nechells Park Hotel public house as it turns into Nechells Park Road on its way back to the city. It is Tuesday 27 February 1940, and with trolleybuses 1 and 3 this vehicle would remain in service until the closure of the route at the end of September. The trio had been overhauled in March 1939, which extended their service lives, so when the 79-90 Class were delivered, the remaining eight half-cab vehicles, 4-11, were made redundant and placed in store.

These 'piano-front' trolleybuses, with their 65hp GEC traction motors mounted beneath the bonnet, ran an average mileage of nearly 182,000 miles in their 8½-year service lives. The Nechells route statistics show that the operation of the route was very intense.

The distant terminus was situated in an area of Victorian housing that adjoined the industrial Tame Valley. The Nechells service was useful as an alternative method of getting to this area; the Erdington group of tram routes travelled through the nearby Salford Bridge on the other side of the Birmingham & Fazeley Canal bridge in Cuckoo Road. *L. W. Perkins*

*Middle* Although some of the Victorian terraced housing remains today in Nechells Park Road, the trolleybus route has significantly altered beyond the Cuckoo Road junction. The last remnants of the old order to remain standing is the renamed Nechells Park public house. Looking beyond the pub towards the former terminus, the old terraces have long since been demolished and replaced with modern factory units, thus expanding the well-established industrial belt in the Tame Valley on to the former residential land. The area is undergoing further change with Cuckoo Road being upgraded to a dual carriageway as part of the Birmingham Heartlands road scheme linking Saltley with Lichfield Road. *D. R. Harvey*

six experimental double-deckers, two in Bradford and four in Leeds, these were the first batch of top-covered vehicles in the country, and within two years Keighley and Nottingham had introduced similar vehicles. The Birmingham examples were instrumental in getting top-deck covers accepted as the norm for petrol-engined buses. *A. D. Packer*

*Right* The same scene today is very different. The 'hucksters' shop in the Victorian terrace has long since gone and on the same site there are six factory units, including the nearest one belonging to Air Products. The change from residential to industrial land use has altered this part of Nechells out of all recognition, and has somehow taken out of the area the feeling of a vibrant community that came with old housing. *D. R. Harvey*

*Below* The smartly dressed driver and conductor pose in front of 'their charge for the day', Railless 4 (OK 4826), at the Cuckoo Road terminus about 1924. The cab of these vehicles was com-

paratively narrow and access was by way of a door on the nearside. Unlike contemporary tramcars, the destination blinds were carried on a single-line roller blind box that was operated from inside the driver's cab.

The impressive acetylene sidelights mounted on the front wings would have been of little value to the driver at night, but at least he did have the luxury of a solitary driving-mirror. The driver had to be admired in that he drove this solid-tyred, hand-accelerated trolleybus on cobbled roads and still had to be aware of the vagaries of the overhead wiring system. After nearly ten years of service these Railless trolleybuses amassed an average of about 260,000 miles before being replaced by the half-cab Leyland TBD1s. *D. R. Harvey collection*

*Below* Leyland TBD1 3 (OV 4003) is seen at the Cuckoo Road terminus on Tuesday 27 February 1940. It has been re-equipped with its original headlights, but they have been masked to comply with the blackout regulations.

When the Second World War began, the 1-11 Class of Leylands and the 12-16 Class of AECs were all operational and had been joined by the last three of the COX-registered Leyland TB5s as the route required more vehicles. With the delivery of the Metro-Cammell-bodied Leyland TB7s of the 79-90 Class in February 1940, all but Nos 1-3 of the half-cab Leylands were withdrawn. These three, including the vehicle shown here, had been given overhauls later than the rest of the class, which led to their retention. It had been previously assumed that the whole of the 1-11 Class continued in service until the enforced closure of the Nechells route in September 1940 took place. *L. W. Perkins*

On the same day, 27 February 1940, Brush-bodied AEC 663T 16 (OJ 1016) stands at the Cuckoo Road terminus similarly decked out in its wartime livery. The five AECs would see service until the closure of the 7 route on 30 September 1940, when they were put into store in Sampson Road paintshop for the duration of the war. They were then sold in June 1945 to Midland Motors of Golden Hillock Road, Sparkbrook, and eventually broken up. In view of the wartime shortage of trolleybuses around the country, their premature withdrawal was surprising. These quite modern-looking vehicles were only eight years old and had covered only an average of about 223,000 miles. *L. W. Perkins*

At least the last three of the COX-registered MCCW-bodied Leyland TB5 trolleybuses were transferred in the summer of 1939 to augment the existing Nechells trolleybus fleet that was operating from Washwood Heath depot. From January 1938 until February 1940, at various times six members of the half-cab 1-11 Class were allocated to Coventry Road depot for peak-hour workings on the Coventry Road service.

Trolleybus 77 (COX 77) is seen at the Cuckoo Road terminus on 24 February 1940. Had the Nechells trolleybus service continued, it is probable that the whole of the 67-78 Class would have been drafted on to the route to augment the AEC 663Ts, as the Leyland TBD1s were coming to the end of their normal life-span and would have been gradually withdrawn. *L. W. Perkins*

This rather uninspired view of the skyline and the chimney pots actually shows the reversing triangle at the Cuckoo Road terminus. Comparatively little is known about this section of wiring as it was only in use for about three years from the time of the opening of the Nechells route in November 1922. *D. F. Potter collection*

A sketch map showing the probable layout of the triangle at Cuckoo Road, which was replaced by the loop at the Long Acre junction about 1925.

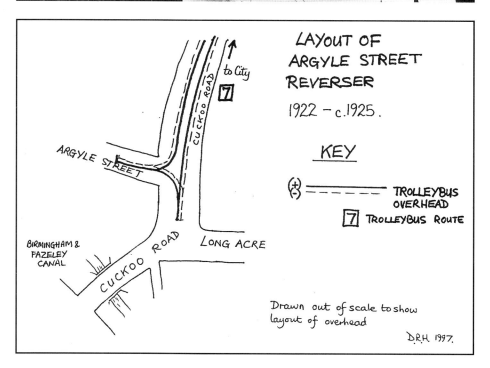

LAYOUT OF ARGYLE STREET REVERSER 1922 – c.1925.

KEY

⊕ ———— TROLLEYBUS OVERHEAD
⊖ – – – –
7 TROLLEYBUS ROUTE

ARGYLE STREET
CUCKOO ROAD
to City
7
BIRMINGHAM & FAZELEY CANAL
CUCKOO ROAD
LONG ACRE

Drawn out of scale to show layout of overhead
D.R.H. 1997.

# Washwood Heath depot

The Nechells route was to remain an isolated outpost of the trolleybus until 1934, when ironically the Coventry Road routes were converted. The opportunity to develop an integrated trolleybus network in the east of the city, with a loop to Small Heath via Bolton Road, had gone when that route was turned over to nor-mal-control Guy single-deckers on 4 February 1930. By that time the pioneering nature of the Railless double-deckers had been superseded by modern petrol buses. Perhaps the attitude towards the trolleybus in Birmingham was summed up by the General Manager, Alfred Baker, who was quoted in 1926 as saying, 'Trolleybuses are only suitable for small towns.'

Railless F12 6 (OK 4828) stands in Washwood Heath depot yard, when new, in November 1922. *Courtesy of Travel West Midlands*

*Right* After the original Roe-bodied Railless vehicles and single-decker AEC demonstrator, the next trolleybus to be delivered was truly revolutionary! No 13 (OL 4636) was the only trolleybus built by the Electro-Magnetic Brake Company (EMB) of West Bromwich. It had a Roe H28/20R body, which was not only top-covered but also had a totally enclosed staircase. The step forward in design was that each of the rear wheels was driven by its own drive-shaft outside the chassis frame. This enabled the chassis height to be extremely low and have a layout similar to the original Bristol 'Lodekka', which was considered to be revolutionary in 1950! Birmingham agreed to operate the trolleybus on a trial basis and if, after 20,000 miles of service, it was successful, BCT would purchase it at an agreed cost of £1,925. It ran in service for only 22 months and was eventually returned to EMB in June 1928 and quietly broken up. It remained unique because although the design was years ahead of its time, rapid strides were taking place with other manufacturers and, being a 'one-off', EMB was not able to develop the design.

No 13 is seen in Washwood Heath yard in April 1924, having been exhibited in Nottingham the previous month. *Whitcombe Collection*

*Below* The last group of trackless trolleybuses delivered to BCT were the 14-16 Class of Railless-built vehicles. They were bodied by Short Brothers to an H25/26RO seating capacity and were delivered in March 1926. The origin of the chassis of these three vehicles has been something of a mystery. Shorts had taken over the Railless company in 1923 and introduced its new Railless LF30 chassis, which was built at Short Brothers' Rochester factory. The new vehicles had a low floor height that was only 2 ft 4 in above the ground, hence the designation LF.

An identical-looking vehicle was exhibited at the 1925 Commercial Motor Show in full Birmingham livery, but was rejected by BCT as it had been fitted with foot-controllers and the Birmingham specification was for hand-controllers. It was subsequently replaced by a fourth vehicle, and the show exhibit was sold to Nottingham Corporation, where it became 10 (TO 5011).

No 15 (ON 2826) is seen at the Nechells terminus, prior to entering service in March 1926. *Courtesy of Travel West Midlands*

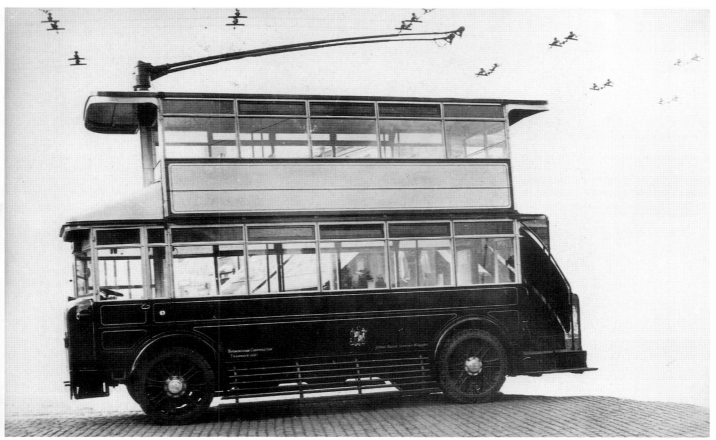

Standing on the forecourt of Washwood Heath depot is an unidentified Short-bodied Railless LF30 of the 14-16 Class. It is 1929, as 787, one of the Brush-bodied EMB air-brake cars that had entered service in the previous year, is visible standing on Road No 4 to the rear of the trolleybus. Roads 7, 8 and 9, obscured by the Railless, were used by the trolleybuses for the 18 years that they worked on the Nechells service. The trolleybus has been painted in the latest bus-style livery, which includes the canopy over the driver's cab being painted cream rather than the original blue. The vehicle is posed with the 'skate' device attached beneath the rear and trailing into the tram track behind it. This skate was used only on depot workings to and from the actual route and eventually led to its closure on 30 September 1940. It was thought that the increase in arcing from the skate would infringe the blackout regulations and therefore be visible to an enemy bomber. *(Courtesy of Travel West Midlands*

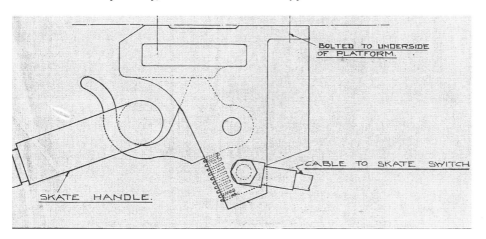

Every Birmingham trolleybus taken permanently into the fleet was fitted with the 'skate' attachment fitted beneath the rear platform. This enabled the trolleybuses to reach the works at Kyotts Lake Road from both Washwood Heath and Coventry Road depots, as well as the everyday movements from Washwood Heath depot to the nearest point of the Nechells route at Bloomsbury Street.

This diagram is dated 10 March 1933 and therefore applies specifically to the vehicles delivered after that date for the Coventry Road services. *Courtesy of D. F. Potter*

*Right* Looking like a contemporary piano-front petrol-bus, Leyland TBD1 stands glinting in the sunshine in the yard of Washwood Heath depot. The impressive Short-bodied trolleybus still has a destination blind, which was later removed in order to save weight and replaced with paper stickers.

No 4 (OV 4013) was, when new, numbered 13, while Railless 4 (OK 4826) still remained in service. At the end of August 1932, when the Railless was withdrawn, the Leyland was renumbered 4, and 15 (OV 4015) became 8. *Courtesy of Travel West Midlands*

*Below left* Again, the rarity value of this photograph makes up for its indifferent quality. The Guy BTX demonstrator is leaving Washwood Heath tram depot and turning into Washwood Heath Road towards the city in February 1930. It is only using the positive wire on the overhead while the return current is earthed through the trailing skate, which is being held in position by one of the depot mechanics as the trolleybus negotiates the pointwork at the exit of the depot. This somewhat dangerous practice, risking a severe electric shock, even with the rubber insulating gloves, would contravene pages of modern-day Health & Safety Regulations, but it must have occurred every day for 18 years if there was a problem passing over the points in the tram track.

The trolleybuses leaving and arriving at Washwood Heath were driven in and out of the yard and were turned around within the confines of the depot forecourt, where they used an extra single piece of tram line in conjunction with an overhead reverser in order to undertake any manoeuvring. *Guy Motors*

*Below right* Also taken from the Guy Motors film of 1930, the Guy-bodied BTX six-wheeled demonstrator, 18 (UK 8341), is seen travelling along Washwood Heath Road from the depot towards The Gate junction at Saltley, and has passed Havelock Road. The 1880s development along Washwood Heath Road was still, at this time, mainly residential, though a canvas awning over a shop front can be seen on the left.

The trolleybus has only the positive pole on the wire and is trailing the skate in the tram tracks. This is the only known film sequence of trolleybuses working between the depot and the Saltley Road junction, where they picked up the trolleybus overhead to gain access to the route in Bloomsbury Street. Passengers were not normally carried on these depot workings, at least officially! Any bound for the city centre would have to catch the 10 tram service and it would have cost them, in 1930, 1½d. *Guy Motors*

*Left* This official Brush photograph of AEC 663T 13 (OJ 1013), attached to a lorry with a towing bar, was taken in the city in September 1932. The problems that the four-wheel Leylands had regarding their weight was overcome by the expedient of ordering six-wheeled vehicles. This also gave the undertaking experience of operating larger vehicles.

These Brush-bodied vehicles were the last composite-construction bodies that Birmingham ordered for its trolleybus fleet. Although this class had many of the features associated with the later metal-framed MCCW-bodied Leylands, the similarity was only skin-deep.

No 13 was used in clearance trials on Coventry Road in the week before the opening on 7 January 1934. In a torrential rainstorm it ran to Yardley and back with sandbags to simulate a passenger load, and was stopped at every request and compulsory stop. This was one of the very few times that one of these AECs ran on Coventry Road. *Brush Coachworks*

*Below left* The enforced closure of the Nechells trolleybus route on 30 September 1940 put all 11 of the half-cab Leyland TBD1s (1-11) off the road, although 4-11 had been stored since 29 February of that year. The five AEC 663Ts (12-16) and Leyland TTBD2s (17-21) joined them in store in Sampson Road paintshop. Whether the intention was to re-introduce them on the Nechells route was ever a realistic one is not known, but by 1944 a considerable amount of the overhead had been taken down and used to repair damaged tram wires elsewhere on the system!

The vacant space in the paintshop had been created in the spring of 1939 when most of the re-painting of the tram fleet was transferred back to Kyotts Lake Road Works. The paintshop was also used during the war to store bomb-damaged tramcars, and ten trams were kept there until the end of the war when the lease on the premises ran out. In fact, only car 744 re-entered service and can be seen on page 22 of Volume 2 of *A Nostalgic Look at Birmingham Trams* working in Bristol Road.

The OC-registered Leylands were returned to service in December 1940, but the 16 earlier trolleybuses never ran again and were sold to Midland Motors of Golden Hillock Road, Small Heath, to be broken up; however, Nos 1 (OV 4001) and 8 (OV 4015), as well as AEC 16 (OJ 1016), were sold to Hollands of Oldbury for scrapping, and the two Leylands were photographed there on 9 June 1950. *D. R. Harvey* collection

*Below right* A 'temporary' replacement bus service, numbered 43, was introduced on 1 October 1940. By 1944 the overhead still remained in place in the Old Square, but the rest of the Nechells trolleybus route was unworkable.

No 1395 (FOP 395), a Guy 'Arab' II with a MoWT-style Park Royal body, had entered service at the end of March 1944 and is turning round at the Old Square terminus in front of a large pre-war Wolseley 25hp car parked near to one of Lewis's sales windows, which is displaying a collection of rather drab, wartime ladies' coats. The bus is fitted with full blackout markings and inside has wooden-slatted seats for its passengers. No 1395 was, however, one of the few wartime buses to receive the luxury of a cream-painted waist-rail. *C. F. Klapper*

# THE
# COVENTRY ROAD
# ROUTES

THE COVENTRY ROAD trolleybus services to Yardley opened on 5 January 1934, and were direct replacements for the two Coventry Road tram routes, the 15 from High Street and the 16 from Station Street. The city terminus of the 15 was altered for the trolleybuses to Albert Street, but with this exception the two routes basically followed the route of the two former tram services.

## A ride along the routes

### City termini: Albert Street

Birmingham's city centre is reached from the south-east by climbing out of the Rea Valley up to the Parish Church of St Martins-in-the-Bull Ring. On their way into the city from Digbeth, the Albert Street trolleybuses passed Rea Street, the site of the Anglo-Saxon settlement that developed at the crossing point of the River Rea and was later to grow into Birmingham. By 1934, when the trolleybuses were introduced, Digbeth had developed into the first shopping centre outside Birmingham's central business area. Digbeth was lined with early-19th-century properties, behind which, in a maze of small streets and alleyways, lay the small factories and workshops that led to Birmingham becoming known as the 'city of a thousand and one trades'.

The trolleybuses bound for Albert Street climbed beyond Moat Row and Digbeth Police Station along a route that was lined, especially on the western side, with warehouses supplying fruit and vegetables for the nearby wholesale markets. These stood in the lee of the Gothic-styled St Martin's. Half way up the hill the road widened out into the Bull Ring, whose southern entrance was guarded by the church.

The trolleybuses, on passing St Martin's and the adjacent loading point for the Midland Red bus services to Coventry, Stratford and Warwick, turned right into Moor Street. This was one of the city's oldest thoroughfares and still had remnants of its more illustrious Georgian past, such as Dingley's Hotel. The trolleybuses proceeded past some rather run-down retail premises and the former Great Western Railway's Moor Street station serving the North Warwickshire line. Alongside the station was Moor Street Warehouse, an imposing Victorian industrial building that stood adjacent to the hump in the road that marked the site of the GWR main-line tunnel into Snow Hill station.

Almost immediately the inbound trolleybuses turned left at the Corner public house into Carrs Lane and climbed towards the city centre to unload at the top of the hill near the junction with High Street.

Passengers were not allowed to travel from here to the loading point, so the by now empty trolleybuses turned right into High Street; after passing the News Theatre, and with the trams in Dale End facing them, they turned right again into Albert Street, where they coasted downhill to the loading shelters outside the Beehive Store. This was the departure point for the 56, 92, 94 and 96 services.

On leaving Albert Street, the trolleybuses turned right into the short one-way section of Moor Street and climbed the short rise, passing the splendid Dingley's Hotel and the rebuilt Carrs Lane Congregational Chapel of 1820, where they met the inbound trolleybuses at Carrs Lane. Approaching the Bull Ring they turned left and descended back into Digbeth.

### City termini: Station Street

The services that used the Station Street terminus were the 57, 93, 95 and 97 routes. These turned left from Digbeth into Rea Street, passing the entrance of the BMMO garage on the right. On reaching Bradford Street they turned right towards the city centre and the markets area, following the tram services that terminated in Hill Street. The trolleybuses then passed the meat market in Bradford Street, which had been opened in 1897, before turning left into Moat Row in front of the impressive Gothic-styled Smithfield vegetable market of 1884. This street was so-called because it followed the line of the moat that surrounded the pre-medieval manor house, which was demolished in 1816.

The trolleybuses continued from Moat Row into Bromsgrove Street where they travelled as far as the Hurst Street junction. This part of the city contained a lot of property that had at one time been residential, but had declined into wholesale, retail and even industrial use.

As the trolleybuses travelled westward along Bromsgrove Street they passed Pershore Street, from which the out-of-city trolleybuses emerged at the end of the one-way trolleybus loop. The right turn from Bromsgrove Street into Hurst Street was the beginning of this one-way trolleybus loop, although the Balsall Heath, Stratford Road and Stechford trams ran in both directions along Hurst Street.

The climb up Hurst Street passed numerous wholesale and retail premises as well as the Birmingham Hippodrome Theatre, with its impressive minaret; further up Hurst Street on the corner of Smallbrook Street was the Empire Theatre, which was opened on 7 May 1894 as the New Empire Palace of Varieties. It was destroyed on 25 October 1940 in an early air raid.

After travelling a short distance along Hill Street the trolleybuses turned right at the Old Crown public house

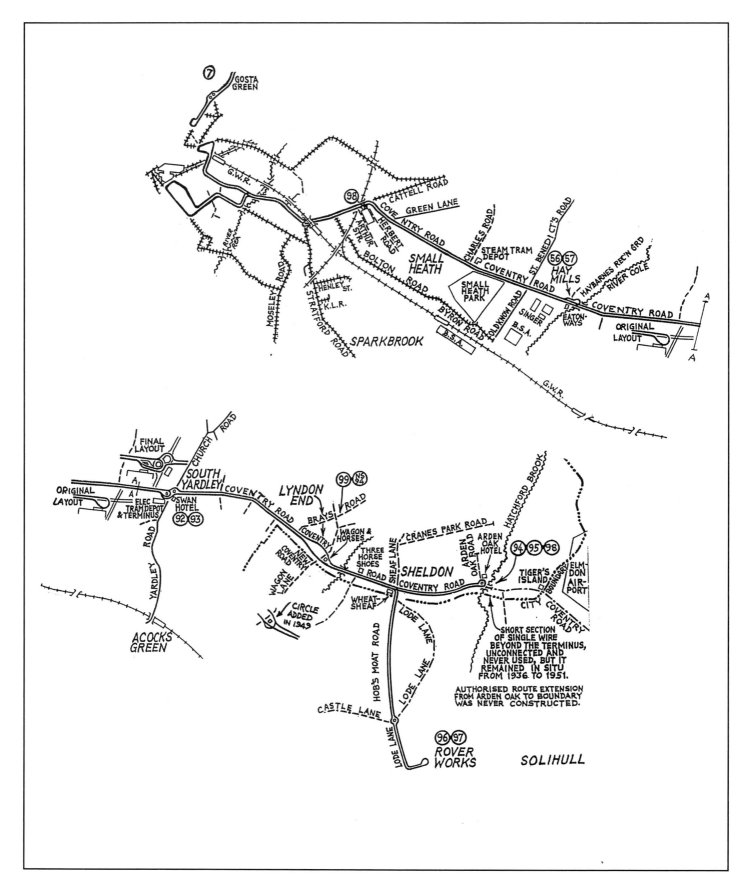

The Coventry Road routes. For an enlargement of the city centre area see the map on page 16.

into Station Street to stop in the shadows of the former Midland Railway side of New Street station.

The imposing shelters in Station Street were left behind as the trolleybuses turned sharp right into Dudley Street at the Market Hotel before crossing Smallbrook Street again on an angled right turn into Pershore Street. This was a bustling area of early-19th-century properties; many of them had been converted into premises that supported the wholesale market trades, selling anything from paper bags to sets of scales. At the end of Pershore Street the trolleybuses turned left into Bromsgrove Street at the end of the terminus loop, then retraced their steps to Digbeth.

## Digbeth to Yardley

Digbeth and Deritend were the former medieval route-ways into the city from Coventry and Stratford and were lined with 18th- and 19th-century buildings. Although around the Rea Street junction there was a shopping centre, beyond that, all the way to the Coventry Road-Camp Hill junction, industrial development dominated the urban landscape. A number of pre-industrial buildings had, however, survived, such as the Crown Inn and St John's Chapel.

The road through Deritend climbed steadily out of the River Rea valley parallel to the former Great Western Railway viaduct as far as the junction with Coventry Road. The trolleybuses coming into the city had the opportunity of turning back towards Coventry Road on an unconnected loop in High Street, Bordesley, immediately after emerging from Bordesley Bridge. This was rarely used after the extension to Sheldon opened, and fell into disuse after the end of the war. The manoeuvre was also extremely awkward, requiring considerable skill by drivers to gain the out-of-city wires.

There was also a short section of unconnected trolleybus overhead around the corner into Camp Hill, which was used from 1934 until 5 January 1937. This enabled trolleybuses to get to Kyotts Lake Road Works by transferring on to the Stratford Road's tram overhead and returning the current by means of a skate attached to the tram track. After this date Coventry Road trolleybuses travelled to Rea Street where they switched to skate operation and travelled by way of Bradford Street and Camp Hill to the works.

The out-of-city trolleybus 92 and 93 routes turned left from High Street, Bordesley, and into the gloom beneath Bordesley bridge, which took the GWR railway line over this busy A45 Coventry Road route. The route then descended across the Watery Lane junction and began the climb up Kingston Hill, passing the imposing Mitchell's paper mill on the left and the former 22 Bolton Road tram route to the right into Bordesley Park Road.

At the top of the hill was Coventry Road depot (also known as Arthur Street). The area in front of the depot was a maze of tram and trolleybus wiring, and was the most complex section of overhead on the entire trolleybus system. The depot, which opened on 24 November 1906, housed all the Coventry Road trolleybus fleet as well as the Stechford tramcars. It saw its last trams leave on 2 October 1948 when the Stechford tram services were converted to bus operation. The replacement buses occu-

pied a much larger space than the trolleybuses and as a result the depot was very congested. Initially some of the replacement Stechford buses had to be operated from the nearby Liverpool Street garage, but eventually land at the rear of Coventry Road garage was taken over and reached via a new door in the back of the building; this allowed buses to be parked in the open, adjacent to Arthur Street. Trolleybuses terminating at the depot displayed either the route number 98 or more usually the prosaic DEPOT ONLY.

The trolleybuses swung to the right in front of the Greenway Arms into Small Heath. The main bustling shopping area along Coventry Road stretched for the next mile past Green Lane, Muntz Street and Charles Road before petering out on the long downward gradient opposite Small Heath Park. This was one of the older parks in the city, being a gift to the town from Miss Louisa Ann Ryland in April 1878. It was also the first area of open green space along the route.

The houses that replaced the 1870s and 1880s Small Heath shop premises were larger and more imposing than previously seen on the route and were the last before the old Yardley UDC boundary was reached. Beyond St Benedict's Road, on the south side of Coventry Road, was the Singer car factory, and behind that was the famous Birmingham Small Arms (BSA) factory complex, which stretched back to the edge of Small Heath Park and was served by the Bolton Road 22 tram route.

At the River Cole bridge at Hay Mills there was another turning circle, only this time it was fully connected. Here, alongside Heybarnes Recreation Ground, was the turn-back for the 56 and 57 trolleybus services. These former tramcar short workings were used mainly in the rush hours for the shift workers at the Singer and BSA factories.

Hay Mills was a mid-Victorian development that had grown up on a much older pre-Industrial Revolution mill site, and became a suburban shopping centre that stretched beyond Kings Road to Deakins Road. After the shopping centre, Coventry Road climbed a long hill, passing the Adelphi Cinema and South Yardley police station on the corner of Holder Road, before reaching the South Yardley terminus at Church Road.

This was the extent of the former 15 tram route to Albert Street and the 16 service to Station Street, which became the 92 and 93 trolleybus services respectively. There was an extensive double loop of wiring at the terminus, put in place after the 1936 extension to Arden Oak Road was opened to enable short working trolleybuses to turn back and enter the Yardley trolleybus 'station'. This was opposite the famous Swan Hotel, and next to the former City of Birmingham Tramways depot, which had opened in 1904 and closed as an operational depot in early 1913.

## Yardley to the city boundary

This extension was opened on Sunday 5 July 1936 and originally ran through nearly open countryside, except for the small hamlet at Lyndon End, to the terminus at Hatchford Brook.

Leaving South Yardley, which as late as 1934 still had the remnants of farm buildings around the junction, the trolleybuses headed eastward along Coventry Road. In the 1930s a ribbon development of semi-detached houses was built between Rowlands Road and Brays Road. In this section of the route the overhead was offset to the northern side of the road. This was the only stretch of trolleybus wiring on the system where two-way working was operated using single-span overhead suspended from a single trolleypole.

After the compulsory stop at the top of the hill at Brays Road, the trolleybuses descended the steep hill in Coventry Road to Lyndon End. This former hamlet at the Barrows Lane junction had a number of early-19th-century cottages, although the large mock-Jacobean Wagon & Horses public house, dating from the 1920s, dominated the area.

The introduction of all-night services in the city occurred on 15 April 1946. The Coventry Road route was operated by buses from Acocks Green garage, and all the night services terminated in the city centre away from the trolleybus overhead. The night service, numbered NS 94A, terminated at Lyndon End, although the destination blinds, confusingly, showed YARDLEY (Wagon Lane), instead of the correct SHELDON! The Wagon Lane turn-back loop, which was the last new section of wiring to be erected, provided the last new route number when the 99 short working was introduced on 24 January 1949 in rush hours, when the Sheldon terminus frequently became congested with trolleybuses.

Trolleybuses coming into the city from either the city boundary or Lode Lane, on reaching Lyndon End, took the southern one-way section and climbed the steady incline of New Coventry Road to meet the outward-bound trolleybuses some half a mile away at the top of the hill at Brays Road.

Continuing out of the city, beyond Lyndon End's old cottages, Coventry Road was again lined by a mixture of late 1930s housing and open space before reaching the small shopping centre clustered around the junction at Sheaf Lane and Hobs Moat Road. This junction was also dominated by another large 1920s public house, the Wheatsheaf Hotel.

Beyond the Wheatsheaf the terminus at Arden Oak Road was over half a mile away. When the trolleybuses were introduced this section of Coventry Road had a concrete-slabbed surface that was unusual in the city, being more typical of the many 1930s trolleybus route extensions elsewhere in Britain. More bay-windowed semi-detached houses were built alongside this stretch of Coventry Road. The houses on the south side were set back from the carriageway, as if anticipating the widening of the road to dual carriageway status that took place many years after the abandonment of the trolleybus route.

## Arden Oak terminus
The terminus for the 94, 95 and 98 services was in a loop at the entrance to Arden Oak Road, just short of Hatchford Brook bridge. A number of shops serving the housing estate were built near to the terminus, which was attractively set among a cluster of willow trees.

The loop was only able to hold two trolleybuses and it was quite normal to see a row of parked vehicles just short of the loop waiting their turn to enter the turning circle before going back to the city. In post-war years

there was usually a caravan parked on the grass verge to serve refreshments to the trolleybus crews.

Beyond the terminus, out towards the actual city boundary, was a length of wire about 40 yards long, which was used for overhead electrical supply purposes. Powers had been granted to operate the route as far as the boundary at Tiger's Island some 0.4 mile beyond Arden Oak Road. However, there was no suitable turning point and although this was open countryside the land beyond Hatchford Brook was earmarked for the new airport at Elmdon and not for housing. Ironically in West Midlands Passenger Transport Executive days, a loop for buses was constructed near to the club house entrance to Hatchford Brook Golf Course, which was very close to the limits of the 1935 trolleybus powers.

## The Lode Lane branch
A trolleybus route, rather than a motor-bus service, branching off the main Coventry Road route to the newly opened Rover Company's wartime 'Shadow' factory in Lode Lane, built to manufacture aero-engines, was authorised under the Emergency Powers (Defence) Act of 1939 and was opened on 29 October 1941. The significance of running trolleybuses along this new section of route was that it was outside the city boundary in Solihull UDC. Normally this would have been the territory of Midland Red, but attempts to save fuel oil demanded that authority was given to BCT to operate a trolleybus service.

The route turned right at the Wheatsheaf Hotel and into Hobs Moat Road, almost immediately crossing the boundary into Solihull; the trolleybuses travelled away from the junction for about three-quarters of a mile. When the route was first opened, Hobs Moat Road was also known as the Sheldon-Solihull By-Pass. The trolleybuses gently climbed through countryside where the planners had already started to build a few houses prior to the outbreak of war. Hobs Moat Road and Lode Lane were the only stretches of road on which the trolleybuses ever used their headlights at night.

On reaching the traffic island at the southern end of Lode Lane, the trolleybuses continued for about another quarter of a mile until the gates of the Rover factory were reached. Here they turned left into the factory's private road before turning in a large loop to unload and load alongside Rover's heavily camouflaged main factory buildings.

There were two routes, the 96 service to Albert Street, which was rarely used, and the more regular 97 service to Station Street. Originally the route was run only to coincide with Rover's working shifts, but by 1942 the service was altered to accept other non-workforce passengers and had become an hourly service. When the factory shifts were being accommodated the Leyland six-wheelers were drafted in because of their larger seating capacity, but at other times any of the available fleet was employed on the Lode Lane branch.

## Vehicle types used on the Coventry Road routes

Clearance testing along the route before the official opening took place in December 1933. AEC 663T 13 (OJ

1013) did the final proving run with members of the Transport Committee on board, which was the only known occasion that any of these five vehicles were ever seen working on Coventry Road. The 17-66 Class of Leyland TTDB2s, which opened the two routes on Monday 5 January 1934, were always employed on the Coventry Road services throughout their long and reliable 17-year careers. They were joined for seven weeks in February and March 1934 by the Sunbeam MS2 demonstrator, which amassed 1,981 miles on the Coventry Road services before being returned to its manufacturer.

The COX-registered 67-78 batch of Leyland TB5 four-wheelers supplied additional vehicles after the opening of the extension to Sheldon in 1936. Nos 76-78 spent a hec-

tic 12 months allocated to Washwood Heath depot working the higher mileages on the Nechells service, until the route was closed at the end of September 1940. As many as five of the Short-bodied Leyland TBD2s of 1932 were used on peak-hour extras from 1938 until February 1940, but never more than two of these half-cab trolleybuses were allocated at any one time. Their nominal replacements, the Leyland TB7s 79-90 (FOK 79-90), never strayed away from the Coventry Road, even during the seven months between their delivery and the closure of the Nechells route.

Four of the six-wheeled Leylands and one of the TB7s were withdrawn in the early part of 1951, but the remaining 69 trolleybuses in the fleet stayed in service until the final closure on 30 June 1951.

# Albert Street to Rea Street

**The 92 and 94 trolleybus routes started their journey of 7 miles 1,300 yards to Sheldon from the loading point in Albert Street outside the Beehive store; the last privately owned department store in the city, it occupied a large site on the northern side of Albert Street, and was run on very traditional lines until it closed on 29 February 1972. The trolleybuses shared the Albert Street terminus with the Stratford Road group of tram routes until the latter's withdrawal on 5 January 1937, and with the Stechford tram routes, which were abandoned on 2 October 1948. The tram tracks, however, remained in situ as they were one of only three links between the somewhat geographically isolated works at Kyotts Lake Road and the remaining seven groups of tram routes.**

**Leyland TTBD2 46 (OC 1146) waits at the terminus in 1950 before starting off to Sheldon. Behind it is a Daimler CVD6 of the 1756-1843 Class working on the recently introduced 54 service to Stechford.** *W. J. Wyse*

**The 1937 12 Leyland TB5 trolleybuses were delivered, carrying 53-seater MCCW bodies similar to the contemporary examples being built on Daimler COG5 chassis. Trolleybus 74 (COX 74) is seen at the Albert Street terminus in 1950 when working on the 94 route to the city boundary at Sheldon. With only about one year's service left in front of it, this vehicle, last overhauled on 31 March 1950, shows that the trolleybuses were maintained to the usual high BCT standard even at this late stage of operation. In common with the bus fleet, the trolleybuses were fitted from new with lower saloon destination blinds on the offside, but these fell out of use during the war in order to save linen. Unlike the buses, the boxes were not plated over flush to the bodywork, but simply had the glass painted cream.** *W. J. Wyse*

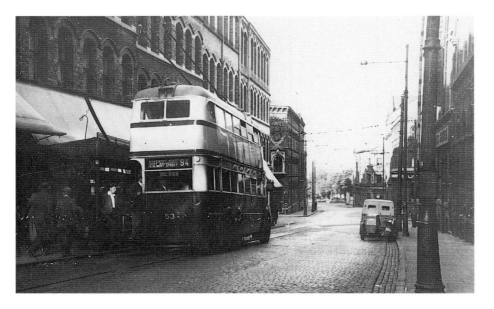

*Top* The Coventry Road trolleybuses left the Albert Street shelters and coasted down the hill before turning right into Moor Street. Six-wheeler 53 (OC 1153) is loading up with passengers at the Beehive shelters in the last year of operation. The trolleybuses, like the trams, never really penetrated Birmingham's city centre; Carrs Lane and Albert Street were as near as the Small Heath shopper could reach directly by public transport.

Albert Street had been partly built in 1851 as a belated link from Birmingham's first railway station at Curzon Street into the town centre. By that time Curzon Street's days as a major railway station were already numbered; opened on 17 September 1838, Philip Hardwick's building with its elegant Ionic portico had a short life, closing to regular passenger services on 1 July 1854 when New Street station was opened. Consequently the development towards the station rather petered out as the need for the road became less important, leaving Albert Street as neither an integral part of the town's shopping centre nor a part of the industrial/warehouse area immediately beyond the central business area. *W. A. Camwell*

*Middle* Leyland TB5 67 (COX 67) inches between MCCW-bodied Daimler CVD6 1829 (HOV 829) and a row of parked cars, which includes, next to the trolleybus, one of the original post-war Morris Minor convertibles and a 1947 Vauxhall Fourteen; opposite the bus are two pre-war Austins, the largest being a Twelve and the leading one an early 1930s Chummy-type Seven.

The bus is loading up at the 53 terminus stand outside Foster Brothers gentlemen's outfitters in Albert Street. The trolleybus is running empty, as per normal, down the street to its loading stop just in front of the Daimler. It is passing the rather brash notices adorning the premises of the Midland Manufacturing Company, who were carpet retailers. *A. B. Cross*

*Bottom* Leyland TTBD2 46 (OC 1146) turns from High Street into Albert Street on the last day of operation. To the right of the trolleybus is Dale End, and behind it is Martineau Street, both of which had seen their last passenger tram services in October 1950 when the Washwood Heath routes closed. The Coventry Road trolleybuses operated a normal Saturday service until 11.00 pm on this last day, and nearly all of the 17-66 Class remained in service until the abandonment. In the lower saloon windows are the notices about the closure of the trolleybus routes and their replacement bus services. It is a tribute to the maintenance standards of the Corporation that there is no evidence of body sag on 46, despite amassing some 519,000 miles in its 18 years of service. *J. Hughes*

*Top* The clock on the wall of the Red Lion pub shows 1.55 pm as Leyland TTBD2 42 (OC 1142) turns from High Street into Albert Street early in 1951. The abandoned tram tracks in the foreground bear testament to the post-war policy of eradicating electric traction from the city. Behind the trolleybus is the News Theatre, opened on 18 January 1932 by Neville Chamberlain to show British Movietone newsreels and cartoons. It finally closed in March 1960, but is indelibly imprinted in the memory because of the travelling illuminated headlines and messages on the canopy.

To the right of the trolleybus are the early-19th-century buildings that stood in High Street between Martineau Street and Union Street. They latterly housed Hilton's ladies fashion shop and Barklays furnishers, but these were demolished in the mid-1950s to be replaced by the Littlewoods store that still occupies the site. *C. Carter*

*Middle* The Austin A40 pick-up van passes the News Theatre in High Street as six-wheeled trolleybus 64 (OC 1164) goes round the loop from Carrs Lane to the terminus in Albert Street. Behind the pick-up is a 1947 Daimler CVA6 working on the 39 route in Dale End. Preedy's Corner, hidden behind the scaffolding, occupied the corner of Bull Street until 1962, while the subterranean gentlemen's toilets, to the left of the trolleybus, is now just a memory in the vitreous eye! *R. Wilson*

*Bottom* The two original trolleybus routes along Coventry Road were a direct replacement of the 15 and 16 tram routes; they ran to the tram terminus at Yardley and were given route numbers 92 and 93 respectively. After July 1936 they became short workings of the extended 94 and 95 routes to Sheldon, although the operation of the 95 service from Station Street was uncommon. Leyland TTBD2 26 (OC 1126), in its original livery with gold lining-out and cream-painted roof, is seen working on a 92 service to Yardley in about 1935. It is passing Pattison's cake shop in High Street. For many years there were three high-class 'tea-rooms' in the city centre, the others being Kunzle, in Union Street, renowned for its chocolate cakes and fancies, and the Kardomah, in Cannon Street, best known for its coffee; the latter had a wonderful Art Nouveau interior and was, in the first decade of the century, where Sybil Thorndike and Lewis Casson did their early courting between theatrical engagements. Pattison's, however, was the place for tea and cakes.

The 27 ft 6 in long MCCW-bodied trolleybuses of the 17-66 Class were the largest order placed in this country at that time for metal-framed trolleybuses. Prior to this BCT order, the bodies had nearly always been of composite construction, ie timber-framed with metal strengthening gussets. Later in 1934 this record was eclipsed when London Transport ordered 350 of its C Class CGF/CUL-registered trolleybuses. *R. Wilson*

The four-wheeled trolleybus deliveries of 1937 and 1940 had a fairly short life compared with vehicles of similar vintage elsewhere in the country. On many other systems 14-year-old Leyland TB5 70 (COX 70), a GEC 80hp-motored vehicle, would have been just about run-in! In this busy summer 1950 scene, No 70 would have only about another year left in service; running empty, it is leaving the Carrs Lane setting-down stop and turning into High Street before returning to Coventry Road depot; passengers were not allowed to be carried between Carrs Lane and Albert Street. Behind the trolleybus is one of the Leyland six-wheelers, an Austin A40 car and an HOV-registered Daimler CVG6 bus of 1949, recently arrived from Hall Green. *V. C. Jones*

The 1934 trolleybuses of the 17-66 Class were employed on the Coventry Road service almost exclusively for the whole of their working lives, and most managed to cover about half a million miles by the time they were withdrawn in June 1951. No 56 (OC 1156) moves away from the terminus in Carrs Lane next to Jays furniture store and travels over the Belisha pedestrian crossing before turning right into High Street. Today the traffic flow in Carrs Lane is reversed with buses travelling away from High Street. *A. D. Packer*

Inbound trolleybuses working into the Albert Street terminus unloaded in Carrs Lane outside Jays store; originally Brodericks shop, it had been built in the 1930s, and in the 1960s the site was redeveloped as part of the Marks & Spencer store. A man looks at the displays of furniture, which by 1951 are beginning to lose their wartime utility appearance; modern styles are being introduced as more luxurious materials become available. Jays is offering low-priced, British-built furniture, though the cost of a new suite would probably be far too expensive for anyone other than the most affluent.

Leyland TTBD2 50 (OC 1150) waits next to traction-pole No 48 and will shortly follow the curve of the tramlines into High Street. Behind is the almost new 2087 (JOJ 87), working on the 50 route. This bus is one of the MCCW-bodied, 'new-look-front' Daimler CVD6s, delivered in the autumn of 1950 to work on the Moseley Road services. *F. Ivey*

Waiting outside Jays in Carrs Lane in 1951 is Leyland six-wheeler 29 (OC 1129), parked at the hexagonal trolleybus stop, which was only used for unloading passengers. After a brief respite it will move round into Albert Street for the next journey out to the city boundary at Sheldon. The 'Vast Exhibition' sign in Jays window doesn't appear to be attracting much interest from the shoppers who seem to be looking at the clothes shop across the road with more enthusiasm! At the bottom of Carrs Lane the driver of one of Acocks Green garage's exposed-radiator Crossleys is about to climb into his cab before leaving on the 44A service along Warwick Road. The climb up Carrs Lane to High Street was quite steep, but the 80hp GEC motor of the trolleybus was more than a match for the 125bhp of the Crossley. A Phase 1 Standard Vanguard is parked outside W. A. Perry's gun shop; this is the only retailer to occupy the same premises today, a reflection of the historic gun trade in the city. *R. Wilson*

Six-wheeled Leyland TTBD2 33 (OC 1133) travels away from Moor Street towards the unloading stop at the top of the hill in Carrs Lane, deserted save for the Morris 8 convertible; it has just turned left at the Corner public house, whose ornamental light can just be seen on the extreme left. Having worked in from Sheldon on the 94 service, 33 is about to pass the wrought-iron bus shelters, the nearest being for the Hall Green 37 route. At the next stop is one of Acocks Green garage's Crossley DD42/7s working on a service to Acocks Green. The advertising hoarding on the left hides a bomb site created by a severe air raid on 9 April 1941. One of the posters advertises a Birmingham Hippodrome production of a variety show entitled *Starlight Roof*, starring the comedy double-act of Jimmy Jewell and Ben Warris. *R. Wilson*

Tram 450, the last of the 50 UEC-built, air-and-oil brake four-wheelers, turns from Albert Street into Moor Street, working on the 42 route during the last year of operation along Moseley Road. The Salvation Army Hostel is dwarfed by the shops and warehouses in Albert Street, while opposite are the canopied loading stands seemingly sprouting out of the Beehive store. Waiting to leave the loading-up stop in Albert Street, behind the illegally parked 1948-registered Standard 8, is trolleybus 75 (COX 75). This 53-seat, MCCW-bodied Leyland TBS entered service on 22 September 1937; the TB5 model was Leyland's standard four-wheeled trolleybus from 1937 until 1939. No 75 is working on the 92 service as far as the old tram terminus at the Swan, Yardley, and will follow the tram to turn right into the narrow one-way section of Moor Street towards Carrs Lane. *W. A. Camwell*

Another of the ubiquitous Leyland six-wheelers, 62 (OC 1162), with a somewhat battered front apron, climbs Moor Street on the short working 56 service to Hay Mills, which was a direct replacement of the same-numbered tram service. It has just passed New Meeting Street and Dingley's Hotel; the latter lovely old building dated from the reign of George II and had Georgian-style architraved windows and a Doric-arched porch with a pilastered entrance, but was demolished in 1962 as it stood in the way of the Inner Ring Road scheme! Nearly all the cars on the right, led by the 1934-registered Morris 8, date from before the war and would be a real prize today for any car preservationist. The same could be said for JOL 261, a 1949 Austin Devon, whose vaguely 1940s American styling was soon to look dated. The design became famous as a very expensive children's pedal-car, given Royal approval by HRH Prince Charles. *A. B. Cross*

When first delivered in 1934, the MCCW-bodied Leylands were extremely modern-looking vehicles, although the design was let down a little by the styling of the front profile below the windscreen and also the lower saloon panels split by beading that had echoes of the old tram-car rocker-panels. However, they represented a period of confident body-styling that was to have a lineage on Birmingham buses through to October 1954, when the last half-cab bus, 3227 (MOF 227), was delivered to the Corporation. The general design of these trolleybus bodies was also found on the solitary Guy 'Arab', 208 (OC 8208), and the 47 Morris 'Imperial' chassis numbered 507-553 (OC 507-553). Later bodies, built by MCCW and BRCW, had very thick upper saloon corner pillars; this gave the buses their Birmingham look, but it was really a retrograde step in body design.

Fully lined-out Leyland TTBD2 35 (OC 1135) works along Moor Street on the original 92 route en route to Yardley. In this 1935 scene it is being followed by an almost new Morris Ten-Four. In the background, just behind the former GWR Moor Street station, is the tall Moor Street Warehouse. All the buildings behind the trolleybus were swept away in the post-war redevelopment of the Bull Ring area, while the Warehouse was gutted in a fire in the early 1960s. *R. Wilson*

A rather mud-splattered, de-poled Leyland TTBD2 19 (OC 1119) is parked in Moor Street about 1949 in its final plain blue livery. The north side of Moor Street was lined by some real architectural gems dating from the turn of the 19th century, although they unfortunately suffered from many years of neglect. In the post-war years it was often fashionable to demolish everything and replace unloved buildings with at best a concrete box, or even worse, as in this case, a new road, cut through about ten years after this photograph was taken. *S. N. J. White*

*Top* Trolleybus 32 (OC 1132) has turned right into Moor Street after climbing the Bull Ring and is approaching a hexagonal trolleybus request stop bearing the words 'To City'; beneath it is a round bus stop for the services that terminated in Carrs Lane. During a shift the conductor on the tram, bus or, in this case, trolleybus rarely needed to turn the destination blind, so it was by means of the stop signs that intending passengers knew which way the vehicle was travelling! Birmingham's municipal transport fleet might have confused intending passengers, especially those from outside the city, as vehicles carried the same destination display in both directions, yet the system was amazingly logical! All the passenger had to do was to look at the stop to see in which direction they were travelling. Well, Brummies understood it!

To the rear of No 32 is Oswald Bailey's Army & Navy Stores, while across the Bull Ring, dwarfing the Midland Red MCCW-bodied AEC 'Regent' of the AD2 Class, is the Woolworth building, closed in October 1962. Behind the Belisha beacon are the railings around the statue of Lord Nelson, paid for by the grateful citizens of Birmingham in 1809 and the first memorial in the country to the Admiral, predating Nelson's Column in Trafalgar Square by some 34 years. *R. Wilson*

*Middle* The trolleybus in Britain was often regarded as being a second-rate vehicle, having neither the prestige or capacity of a tram nor the manoeuvrability of a bus. They emerged silently from side streets, sped along main roads with admirable frequency and retired into contemporary interwar suburbia. There is an element of truth about this regarding the Coventry Road routes, with their 2-minute headway.

Two Leyland TTBD2 trolleybuses, 27 (OC 1127) and 35 (OC 1135), are in Moor Street approaching the left turn into the Bull Ring on their way out of the city on the 94 service to Sheldon. No 27, leading, is about to leave the stop outside Nelson House and pass Allen Griffiths's shoe shop on the corner of the Bull Ring. A sign on one of the first-floor windows advertises True Vue Television. By 1951 the influence of the BBC's Sutton Coldfield transmitter, opened on 17 December 1949, was beginning to attract customer attention. *R. Wilson*

*Bottom* Taking the difficult left turn from Moor Street into the Bull Ring is trolleybus 68 (COX 68), the second of the 12 Leyland TB5s delivered in September 1937. Their MCCW bodies were similar to the contemporary Daimler COG5 diesel bus, but because of the extra weight of the traction motors, batteries and trolley-pole gantry, at 7 tons 6 cwt, they were half a ton heavier than the Daimler. Rather like the half-cab TBD1s before them, the 1937 trolleys would have fallen foul of the weight regulations had their seating capacity not been only H29/24R.

Behind the trolleybus is the rather faded premises of Oswald Bailey. In the years after the war this shop did sell genuine surplus apparel, which was hard-wearing, cheap and totally unfash-

ionable! This, of course, was years before the Bailey chain was absorbed into the House of Fraser group and became a shop specialising in outdoor clothes and camping gear. The shop was demolished in 1961 when the elegant decaying grandeur of the Moor Street buildings was swept away in the Bull Ring redevelopment scheme. *M. J. C. Dare*

**Top** Leyland TB7 trolleybus 83 (FOK 83) turns out of Moor Street into the Bull Ring in the spring of 1951. The steepness of the hill combined with the cobbled sets on the road surface made the Bull Ring extremely hazardous, especially in wet and icy conditions. While the content of the grit bin, labelled NO BILLS, was of some value in poor weather, the hill could prove too much for some of its users, such as the young lad on his bicycle. To his left and parked in front of St Martin's Parish Church is a BMMO D5 waiting to work its next duty on the 148 route to Evesham.

At the top of the distant Bull Ring, to the left of the almost new 'new-look-front' Daimler CVD6 on the cross-city 29A route from Hall Green to Kingstanding, is the old Market Hall, with its impressive Doric-order main entrance. Designed by Charles Edge and officially opened on 12 February 1835, it stood between Bell Street and Phillip Street, was 365 feet long by 106 feet wide, and could hold up to 600 stalls selling fresh fruit and vegetables, meat, poultry and fish. In the adjacent Bell Street the overwhelming smell of fish from the wholesale fish market was more akin to the docks at Lowestoft. The Market Hall was partially destroyed in the air raid during the night of 25-26 August 1940, only the outer walls being left standing. This historic building continued to serve as Birmingham's main retail market until it was demolished in 1962. Even then, despite the previous attentions of the Luftwaffe, explosives had to be used to finally pull it down. *F. Lloyd*

**Middle** The climb up the Bull Ring from Digbeth posed very little problem for the 80hp GEC-motored Leyland four-wheelers. An almost full 76 (COX 76) follows the tramlines into Moor Street as it comes into the city on a 94 service. Following is a Wolseley 18/85 car, while descending the Bull Ring in the distance is a Daimler COG5 on the 44 route to Acocks Green.

One of the forgotten social habits of the time was to cover the head. Until the 1950s it was accepted that men wore a cap, a trilby or even a bowler hat. The headscarf, as seen here being worn by the mother and grandmother holding the hand of the little girl, was the traditional headgear of housewives and working women. The woman to the left, in the twin-set, might have been considered under-dressed except that this was obviously a warm day, as revealed by the number of open windows on the trolleybus. *C. Carter*

**Bottom** The imposing Victorian Gothic Parish Church of St Martin dwarfs the other buildings around it as trolleybus 47 (OC 1147), one of the 27 ft 6 in, short-wheelbase Leyland six-wheelers, turns out of Moor Street into the Bull Ring before descending towards Digbeth. Ahead of it is a Standard 8 car and ascending the hill is another of the MCCW-bodied 17-66 Class. This rear view shows the access steps to the trolleypoles on the rear dome as well as the typical Power Brake triangular light below the rear window. *R. Wilson*

*Top* The pipe-smoking man nearly obscures trolleybus 90 (FOK 90), numerically Birmingham's last trolleybus, as it begins the ascent of Digbeth on its way to the Bull Ring; working on the 94 route, it has just passed Moat Lane. Buildings alongside the trolleybus were destroyed in air raids, which accounts for the two sets of gable-end advertising hoardings. Exide car batteries, Swan Vestas matches, Dunlop tyres and Wrigley's chewing-gum are all brand names that survive 45 years later.

The climb up to the Bull Ring was quite steep and served as a reminder that in medieval times a castle for defensive purposes or, as in Birmingham, the village church, as St Martin's had been, was always built at the top of a hill, so that the worshippers would be 'nearer to heaven'. *A. B. Cross*

*Middle* After descending the Bull Ring, the trolleybus, bus and tram services passed the Lightfoot Refrigeration Company Ice Works, the tall brick building behind the trolleybus on the corner of Allison Street. On the extreme right is Digbeth Police Station, opened in 1911. Nearly empty Leyland trolleybus 33 (OC 1133) approaches the junction with Meriden Street on the 94 route, closely followed by a semi-forward-control, London-registered Morris-Commercial Equiload 2-ton van and a Morris 8 car of about 1948 vintage.

The trolleybuses had at last, 18 years after their introduction in Birmingham, a road to themselves! The tram tracks in the foreground were by 1950 only used for journeys to the tram repair works in Sparkbrook. However, within 12 months the Coventry Road trolleybus routes would be withdrawn and the trams would continue to run for another two years. Birmingham was the only operator in Britain to replace its trolleybus services before the abandonment of its trams. *A. B. Cross*

Despite all the redevelopment that has altered Birmingham's city centre, parts of the Digbeth area still retain their pre-war character. Preserved ex-BCT Crossley 2489 (JOJ 489) passes the police station in a scene that has hardly changed since 1950. The same could not be said of the Bull Ring; the 24-storey, 271-foot cylindrical Rotunda office block, opened in 1965, forms a focal point that dominates the skyline. What is perhaps most noticeable about this view, taken on Sunday 21 July 1996, is that the amount of Sunday traffic today exceeds the normal weekday traffic of 1950. This was realised by the photographer and Barry Ware, who was driving the Crossley, as this 'then and now' photograph was extremely difficult to take! *D. R. Harvey*

In 1934 the Digbeth-Deritend route out of the city was a very different looking road from that of today, being lined with 18th- and 19th-century buildings such as Wiseman's drapers store at No 91 Digbeth. Parked in front of it is a rather solid-looking four-door, six-cylinder Morris Major car built about 1931.

Leyland TTBD2 63 (OC 1163) is travelling towards the city on the 92 route from Yardley; it was unique in the 17-66 Class as it had ventilation slots in the dome above the upper saloon front windows. It is painted in its original gold-lined-out livery style, carried until it received its fifth repaint in July 1949. Two years later it would be consigned to Bird's scrapyard after running a total of 508,380 miles in service. *J. Cull*

Leyland TTBD2 trolleybus 62 (OC 1162) of 1934 passes the Mitchells & Butlers-owned Old Bull's Head public house in Digbeth in 1950.

These buildings on the east side of Digbeth survive today, while those on the west side were demolished when the road was widened in July 1955. This scheme had been proposed in the late 1930s and would have caused the abandonment of the Moseley Road and Stechford tram services, but the outbreak of war led to the suspension of the scheme, and by the time the trolleybuses had disappeared from the streets of Birmingham, it had still not taken place. *S. E. Letts*

The junction of Rea Street and Digbeth was the most important on the Coventry Road group of trolleybus routes. The services to Station Street turned left into Rea Street, following the by now redundant tram tracks, and passed Midland Red's Digbeth garage.

In 1951 four-wheeled trolleybus 76 (COX 76), a 1937-delivered MCCW-bodied Leyland TB5, passes Digbeth Institute on the 94 route, followed by one of the sophisticatedly quiet but oil-burning Daimler CVD6s, 1945 (HOV 945), which is working on the 50 route to the Moseley Road, also via Rea Street. *R. T. Wilson*

# Station Street to Rea Street

*Top* The third city terminus on the Birmingham trolleybus system was the least known, being tucked away behind New Street station in Station Street, and the most remote from the central shopping area. It had inherited its loading point from the 16 and 57 tram routes.

Station Street had been created in 1883 when the Midland Railway took over a large area of 18th-century property that lay to the south side of Queens Drive and the original LNWR station. The MR station was built over the existing street pattern, and as a by-product of this development removed some of the worst housing in Birmingham.

Nearly new Leyland TTBD2 50 (OC 1150) stands at the 93 route stop. The front wheels have just a hint of right-hand lock, so that the driver could haul his 8 ton 17 cwt trolleybus into Dudley Street and out of the city via the markets area.

Note the advertisements on the wall of the station for Swan Vestas and Virol tablets, the latter a sort of 1930s Prozac. Towering above the station in the background are the curious 'portholes' of the Futurist cinema in Hill Street, opened on 30 July 1919 and the first city centre cinema to show a sound film; this took place on 18 March 1929 and the film was *The Singing Fool* starring Al Jolson. *R. T. Wilson*

*Middle* The 50 six-wheel Leyland trolleybuses led an arduous life on the Coventry Road routes, most running over half a million miles in their 17-year service life. They were a very sound investment at a time when metal-framed bodies on trolleybuses were still something of a novelty. Wearing its years remarkably well, trolleybus 20 (OC 1120) stands in Station Street in 1949 prior to leaving on the 93 service to Yardley. This was one of five of the Coventry Road trolleybuses withdrawn as surplus to traffic requirements after the suspension of the Nechells service; Leylands 17-21 spent just over two months in store at Sampson Road paintshop before being restored to service in early December 1940. *S. N. J. White*

*Bottom* Former Birmingham City Transport Crossley DD42/7 2489 (JOJ 489), fitted with a trolleybus blind displaying the 93 route to Yardley, stands in approximately the same place opposite the Market Hotel in July 1996. The rebuilding of New Street station between 1963 and 1967 totally changed the appearance of Station Street's north side, and part of the station can be seen behind the Crossley. Ironically all the buildings on the south side of Station Street from Hill Street to Dudley Street have survived. This 'island' of turn-of-the-century buildings includes the original Birmingham Repertory Theatre; founded by Sir Barry Jackson, it opened on 15 February 1913 with a production of *Twelfth Night*. *D. R. Harvey*

*Top* Although built to full pre-war standards, trolleybus 84 (FOK 84) had entered service on 20 February 1940 and belonged to the class of 12 vehicles that were intended to replace all the half-cab Leyland TBD1s of 1932; they were the last trolleybuses to enter service with Birmingham City Transport. The 79-90 Class were very advanced for their time, being fitted with traction batteries; the previous 67-78 Class had similar equipment that allowed them to manoeuvre away from the overhead.

The only time that Birmingham's trolleybuses ever carried advertisements was during the Second World War, and they were always for National Savings Certificates. As well as this advertisement, trolleybus 84 has all the wartime embellishments.

It is a little surprising that other than the 1939 FOF-registered, MCCW-bodied Daimler COG5 working on the 36 route to Stechford, the only other vehicle in Station Street is a private car, a Morris 12. The wartime privations, including severe petrol rationing, made it unusual to see a privately owned car on the road, particularly at this period of the war. *R. T. Wilson*

*Middle* The last trolleybus to enter service in Birmingham was 90 (FOK 90), and during the last year of operation it was frequently used for enthusiasts' tours. It is seen in June 1951 parked some distance short of the terminus stop in Station Street with its tour driver and gaberdine-carrying trolleybus enthusiasts. After leaving the terminus it turned right into Dudley Street at the Market Hotel. The twin-traction poles that straddled the Dudley Street turn are visible behind the Austin Ten-Four parked outside the Repertory Theatre on the right. The nearest canopy belongs to the Tatler News Cinema, the first purpose-built cinema in Birmingham, opened on 30 July 1910.

Station Street was gradually run down as a city terminus for Corporation buses. The top end was used extensively by Midland Red on its routes to Burton, Evesham, Lichfield and Worcester. In the distance, below the porticoed-entrance to the Market Hall, are two BMMO S9 under-floor-engined single-deckers and a D5 double-decker on the 147 service to Redditch. *J. H. Meredith*

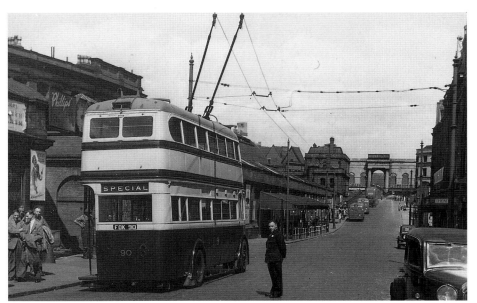

*Bottom* Inbound trolleybuses from Digbeth going to Station Street travelled via Bradford Street, Moat Row and Bromsgrove Street. Leyland TTBD2 32 (OC 1132) waits to turn right into Hurst Street at the traffic lights in Bromsgrove Street outside A. D. Wimbush's bread shop, at the head of a queue of traffic that contains an Austin K4 lorry and a much larger, mid-1930s Leyland 'Beaver'. The row of buses includes a recently delivered 2181 Class Leyland 'Titan' PD2/1 with a Park Royal body, one of Yardley Wood garage's Brush-bodied Leyland PD2/1s working to Ethel Street, and an FOF-registered Daimler COG5.

Above the trolleybus are the twin trolleybus wires with a third, single wire for trams; the Moseley Road and Stechford tram services had been abandoned by this time, and Bromsgrove Street was used only by Selly Oak and Cotteridge depots for works journeys to Kyotts Lake Road by way of the remnants of the former Stratford Road tram route.

The trolleybus is working on the 93 service from Yardley; even at this late stage of its career, with only one year of service to go, the blue paintwork on its lower panels still sparkles in the sunlight. *R. T. Wilson*

*Top* It is June 1951 and MCCW-bodied Leyland TB7 87 (FOK 87) negotiates the 'Keep Left' bollards as it crosses Smallbrook Street and turns into Pershore Street, having emerged from Dudley Street in the foreground. It is working on the 93 to Yardley. The four-storeyed Sydenham Hotel dominates the junction and appears to be a permanent feature of the back-street market landscape through which the trolleybus is passing. However, the transient nature of urban landscapes is well demonstrated in this view: Smallbrook Street would vanish by 1960 with the construction of the Inner Ring Road, and with it would go the Sydenham Hotel. The Vauxhall 12/4 car of 1948 would probably fall victim to the 1958 MOT regulations, the trolleybus service would be abandoned at the end of the month, and the whole of the scene would disappear within the next 12 years. It was rumoured that these 11-year-old Leyland TB7 trolleybuses were going to be exported as chassis to South Africa, but in the event all 12 were sold to W. T. Bird of Stratford for scrap, although two of the bodies were used again. *R. Wilson*

*Middle* The last of the 50 metal-framed Leyland TTBD2 trolleybuses, 66 (OC 1166), speeds past the plodding horse-drawn cart in Pershore Street when working on the 93 service to Yardley in the summer of 1934. This is the only known photograph of a Birmingham trolleybus in Pershore Street and is included for its rarity value.

The trolleybus is equipped with the twin-roller-type windscreen wipers that were fitted to all the bus and trolleybus fleet in the 1930s. The vehicle is painted in the original gold-lined pre-war livery with the roof painted cream. *J. Cull*

*Bottom* The services that started in Station Street left the markets area by way of Moat Row and Bradford Street before turning left into Rea Street. In June 1951 Leyland TTBD2 30 (OC 1130) is about to turn right from Rea Street into Digbeth on an out-of-city 93 service to Yardley, and has just passed the entrance to the Digbeth garage of Midland Red, the two large entrance doors of which can be seen behind the stop on the right.

Following the trolleybus is a BR Scammell 'mechanical horse' three-wheel lorry, developed in 1930 by the London, Midland & Scottish Railway specifically for short-haul transfer journeys to and from goods yards. The design was developed by Karrier of Huddersfield, with the Cob tractor unit. The Scammell design originated in 1933, and they became the mainstay of the railways' local road freight transfer work. The last design was the post-war Scammell Scarab, which fell foul of revised regulations that required all wheels to be equipped with brakes. As all these three-wheelers only had brakes on the rear axle, the Scammells virtually disappeared overnight from railway work. On the left is an almost new Guy 'Arab' IV of the 2526 class working on an inbound 44A service from Acocks Green *R. Knibbs*

*Above* The five-storey factory of Goodman & Sons, engravers and letter manufacturers, dwarfs the corner of Milk Street and the junction between Digbeth, in the foreground, and High Street, Deritend. The Metro-Cammell-bodied Leyland TB5, 74 (COX 74), has just coasted beneath the power cables that can be seen coming from the second traction pole on the right. The driver has to exercise considerable care as, if he crosses places where the power comes into the overhead with the trolleybus accelerating, he will blow the cab resistors and the trolleybus will grind to an undignified halt. No 74 is returning to the city from Yardley and will turn left into Rea Street and proceed to Station Street. The conductor has used the 'pull-frog' lever near the junction to enable the trolleybus to negotiate the turn.

Following the Austin 10 behind the trolleybus and about to overtake the parked Standard Vanguard Phase 1 is an EOG- or FOF-registered Daimler COG5 working on a 54 route from Stechford. The bus has just passed over the culverted River Rea, which was the original settlement site for the Anglo-Saxon hamlet that grew to become Birmingham. The Big Bull's Head public house was an Atkinson's Brewery hostelry; Atkinsons were based in Queens Road, Aston, near Aston Hall. *W. A. Camwell*

# Digbeth to Kingston Hill

The BCT trolleybus system lasted long enough into the post-war years to overlap into the era of underfloor single-deckers and the 'new-look-front' designs of double-deckers. Here 1934-built Leyland TTBD2 trolleybus 19 (OC 1119) is followed past the Rea Street junction by a BMMO underfloor-engined S12 type on a 186 service from Barston and Knowle.

To the left of the trolleybus, having just turned out of Rea Street into Digbeth on the 15A route, is BCT 2427 (JOJ 427), the second vehicle in the batch of 100 'new-look-front' Crossley DD42/7s with Crossley-built bodies. Like all new post-war buses it has the khaki-painted roof that was introduced during the war as a camouflaging feature; the khaki paint was considered to be far more durable than the previous pre-war cream-liveried roofs. *A. B. Cross*

Picking up passengers outside Fowler's ironmongers shop in May 1934 is Leyland six-wheeler 64 (OV 1164). On a cold day passengers could have made for the shop next door, which was William Brown's coffee house, for a delightful cup of BEV or Camp coffee! The trolleybus is working into the city terminus at Albert Street on a 92 service from Yardley, while about to turn out of Rea Street into Deritend on a 93 service is another of the same 17-66 Class. It is waiting in front of the 'SPQR' store, whose initials were corrupted from the Latin meaning to 'Small Profits and Quick Returns'. The shop was the 1930s equivalent of a cross between Cantors and B&Q! Behind the blurred trolleybus is a 702 Class totally enclosed tram, which has just turned out of Rea Street into Digbeth on its way to Albert Street on one of the Moseley Road routes. *D. R. Harvey collection*

Leyland TB7 84 (FOK 84) crosses the Rea Street junction in Digbeth working an inbound 94 service. The TB7 model was a rare Leyland trolleybus type; only West Hartlepool and Kingston-upon-Hull took this model before production ended in 1940. No 84 is followed by an exposed-radiator Daimler CVD6 on a 54 service from Stechford. These Daimler CVDs were among the quietest and most sophisticated diesel-engined double-deckers ever owned by BCT, but were also heavy consumers of engine oil. Travelling out of the city on the 94 route is six-wheeled trolleybus 38 (OC 1138).

The original alignment of the buildings in Deritend can be seen alongside trolleybus 84, including Ridgway's shop on the corner of Rea Street, which appears to be selling crockery whereas in earlier years they had been manufacturers of tubular steel furniture. Behind the Standard Flying Nine car is the Phosphor Bronze Company's factory, built in the 1930s and set back from the original road to enable the proposed rebuilding of Digbeth/Deritend into a dual carriageway. *R. Wilson*

MCCW-bodied six-wheel Leyland TTBD2 42 (OC 1142) approaches Rea Street on a learner duty in 1950. Driver training took place on the Coventry Road route interspersed with the normal service until the spring of 1951. As trolleybuses came under railway regulations, learner drivers could drive their vehicle in passenger-carrying service. Elsewhere in the country this was often the normal practice, but in Birmingham it was not! The second trolleybus is 63 (OC 1163), the only one of the 17-66 Class to have ventilators in the front dome, which is working on the 94 service. *A. B. Cross*

**Top** While the River Rea bridge was being rebuilt in the spring of 1937, it became necessary to use the open space in front of the newly built Phosphor Bronze Company's factory as a diversion. During this period one of the OC-registered six-wheelers negotiates the temporary wiring while working into the city on the 92 route.

Behind the trolleybus is the tower of St John the Baptist Chapel. A church of this name had been on this site since 1375 and this Italian-styled building dated from its 1777 reconstruction. It was severely damaged in an air raid in 1940 and demolished in 1948 in order to facilitate the intended road widening of Deritend. *Birmingham Public Works Collection*

**Middle** The livery changes necessitated by the introduction of blackout regulations at the outbreak of the Second World War included camouflaging the roof with khaki paint, masking the headlights (so that the only light emitted was cast downwards), and painting the bottom edges of the vehicles white. Leyland TTBD2 64 (OC 1164) speeds along Deritend High Street on its way to Bordesley on 9 June 1940 on the infrequently worked 95 route; the service from Station Street to the city boundary at Sheldon was usually covered by 94 route workings from Albert Street, while most Station Street turns terminated at Yardley as 93s. No 64 is equipped with the patented double-chain windscreen wipers, designed by Mr Rowlands, who was BCT's Chief Engineer, and Mr Parker. These two gentlemen patented a number of designs marketed by Clayton Dewandre, such as the RP Brake Adjuster.

The trolleybus has passed the Phosphor Bronze Company's factory, while to the left is the soon to be bombed St John the Baptist Chapel. The slight rise in Deritend over the River Rea bridge can be seen. *J. H. Taylforth collection*

**Bottom** One of the oldest buildings to survive to the present day in Birmingham is The Old Crown in Deritend. Built in 1368 as a mansion house, by 1700 it had become the first coaching inn in the town. The splendid Elizabethan half-timbered, jettied front was spoilt by the 1862 additions to the rear of the old inn in Heath Mill Lane. Unfortunately at the time of writing The Old Crown is empty and boarded up, although under restoration.

In 1937 MCCW-bodied Leyland TTBD2 trolleybus 24 (OC 1124) travels past the pub on its way to the city on the 93 route. The trolleybus will descend through the industrial area of Deritend, which was seen in 1538 by the English antiquarian John Leland, who described 'Dertyend' as 'as pretty a street as ever I entered'. Parked outside the pub is a 1937 Singer Bantam saloon. *D. R. Harvey collection*

*Top* The 2-minute frequency of the trolleybus service along Coventry Road was maintained because of the high passenger loadings throughout the day. Leyland TB5 67 (COX 67) has a 'three-bell' load, and as a result appears to be very low on its springs. Conductors had a bell-code that told the driver exactly what was required: one bell was stop, two was go, three was 'full up and keep going', while four denoted trouble and that there was some sort of emergency.

The four-wheeler has just pulled away from the hexagonal trolleybus stop near the Alcester Street junction in High Street, Bordesley. The wartime Guy 'Vixant' lorry travelling out of the city is passing Frank Plant's newsagents, which is advertising, as part of his shop's name sign, the *Radio Times*, which by this date would have been advertising the early BBC television programmes being produced from Lime Grove in London and transmitted from the Sutton Coldfield transmitter, opened on 17 December 1949. *S. E. Letts*

*Middle* Beyond The Old Crown, Deritend climbed steadily towards Bordesley. About halfway between these two points was the Alcester Street junction, which even in 1949 was controlled by traffic lights and still had the blackout white markings. The rather unwashed and lightly loaded trolleybus, 57 (OC 1157), accelerates through the traffic lights when working on a 94 service to Sheldon. It is passing the mid-19th-century buildings that survive today despite the 1955 reconstruction of Deritend to a dual carriageway. Immediately behind these buildings is the impressive former Great Western Railway's brick viaduct that took the main line from Snow Hill station through Bordesley and on to London; the lack of available land for redevelopment between the buildings and railway has to some extent ensured the former's survival.

To the rear of the Leyland six-wheeler is one of the Birmingham Co-Operative Society's many grocery stores, while overlooking the traffic lights are the offices of Jackson Royle, who provided hardware for the catering trade. *S. N. J. White*

*Bottom* High Street, Bordesley, in 1938 was a rather down-at-heel area. Although the terracotta-fronted Bird's Custard factory dominates the distant skyline, the buildings on either side of the Alcester Street junction are entering their last few years of occupancy, their proposed demolition postponed because of the outbreak of war.

This conflict was being impressed on the population, at the time, as being somehow inevitable. The euphoria after the return of Birmingham's Neville Chamberlain, the Prime Minister, from the meeting with Chancellor Hitler at Munich had, within a few months, worn rather thin. This is demonstrated by the advertisement for men to become ARP Wardens, on the top right of the hoarding, suggesting the feeling that another confrontation was going to be inevitable. An unidentified Leyland TTBD2 is working on the 93 route and is about to leave the hexagonal trolleybus stop opposite The Old Crown public house. *Birmingham Reference Library*

*Above* The junction of High Street, Bordesley, with Camp Hill, to the right, and Coventry Road, to the left, became something of a notorious point for traffic congestion by the end of the 1950s, and from 15 October 1961 was the site of the Camp Hill flyover, which took all the out-of-city Stratford Road traffic. This 'temporary' structure stood for 25 years and was not demolished until 1986!

The last of the 1934 deliveries, 66 (OC 1166), passes the point where the fly-over began its sweep over the junction into Camp Hill. It is working into the city on the 94 service, having just turned out of Coventry Road. It is 1948 and the trolleybus is being followed by a 301 Class tram working on an 84 service from Stechford. Emerging from the gloom of Bordesley railway bridge is one of the 211-295 Class of EOG-registered Leyland 'Titan' TD6cs, on the cross-city 16 route to Hamstead.

On the right is the Fisher & Ludlow factory, which at this time still had the wartime anti-blast walls; realistically these would have offered little protection from a direct hit by a bomb. *J. S. Webb*

*Below left* An unusual piece of overhead wiring on the trolleybus system was to be found in High Street, Bordesley. Trolleybus 31 (OC 1131) is in a loop, turning back towards Coventry Road. The peculiar arrangement was that the overhead did not cross the inbound city line and therefore did not reach the out-of-city overhead. The trolleybuses, if they were successfully using this unconnected loop, had to go right to the end of the wiring, then be re-connected to the out-of-city wiring. At about 13 feet, this was at the maximum reach of the trolleybooms.

The skill of the trolleybus drivers in manoeuvring their vehicles around this strange arrangement has to be admired, especially when it is remembered that the 17-66 Class, with one exception, were not equipped with traction batteries to allow for movements of the wiring. All the four-wheelers, the 1937 67-78 Class and the 1940 79-90 Class were so equipped, but somewhat ironically, by the time that they were delivered this manoeuvre in Bordesley was rarely done. *D. R. Harvey collection*

*Below* A sketch map of the layout of the overhead at Bordesley junction, January 1934 to January 1937. *D. R. Harvey*

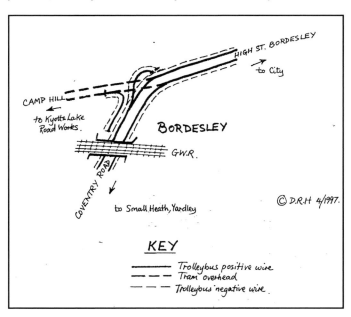

*Above left* As the 1937-registered Austin Cambridge saloon speeds towards Bordesley bridge, Leyland six-wheeler 26 (OC 1126) stands at the hexagonal trolleybus stop on an city-bound 92 working from Yardley to Albert Street in 1951. In the gloom of the former GWR railway bridge is trolleybus 77 (COX 77) on a 94 service to the city boundary. A cyclist is about to pass an Austin A40 Devon saloon, while beyond the bridge can be seen a 'new-look-front' Crossley DD42/7, less than one year old, on its way to Garretts Green.

The trolleybus is standing on the disused tram tracks that had been last used over two years before when the Stechford routes were closed. Above No 26 is a second set of overhead wires; these were never connected to the service wires and trolleybuses turning left into Camp Hill used them on their way for overhaul at Kyotts Lake Road works (see the map opposite). Once round the corner they had to use the tram overhead and a skate to proceed. This method of getting to the works could not be used after 1937 as the tram overhead was dismantled in Camp Hill when the Stratford Road group of tram routes was abandoned.

For many years Bordesley bridge, 'the gateway' into Coventry Road, displayed the advertisement for Maudslay, which had been one of the pioneers of commercial vehicles in this country and had made lorries and buses since 1905. By the time this photograph was taken, Maudslay, as well as Crossley Motors, had been taken over by ACV and both would end vehicle manufacturing. *W. A. Camwell*

*Above right* The bridge appears largely unchanged in this view taken on a quiet Sunday in July 1996. The Maudslay advertisement disappeared not long after the company itself disappeared, and the Dowding & Mills sign has, in various forms, graced the bridge for many years. This well-known Birmingham electrical company today occupies the whole of the site from the bottom of Camp Hill to the corner of Coventry Road.

In the intervening 45 years only a few buildings beyond the bridge have survived various road-widening schemes, although the Clements Arms public house, the white building, is still there. Today the Middle Ring Road bisects Coventry Road beyond the bridge and takes through traffic along the A45 away from Small Heath via the Small Heath Highway. *D. R. Harvey*

*Below* Standing in the stygian gloom of Bordesley bridge in 1951 is MCCW-bodied Leyland TTBD2 20 (OC 1120). The young boy runs past the premises of Barnett's furniture re-upholsterers, which occupied one of the railway viaduct arches as the trolleybus quietly hums before the driver accelerates from the stop on its way out of the city.

The arches still serve today as the premises for many small companies. Although the trolleybuses, the cobbled road and the tram tracks have long since gone, the scene remains much the same today as 2489 (JOJ 489) stands in the shadows on 21 July 1996 showing the trolleybus destination 94 on its blind.

The derelict tram lines were lifted years ago and Bridge News now occupies Barnett's premises. It would be interesting to know what happened to the young lad; it is a sobering thought that if he is still alive he will be in his late fifties! *R. Wilson/D. R. Harvey*

**Above** Five years after the abandonment of the trolleybus service, Coventry Road looked virtually the same except that the road had been tarmacked. On Tuesday 8 May 1956 an almost new Austin A40 Somerset crosses the Sandy Lane junction on its way into the city while a Morris Commercial CV lorry waits in Watery Lane for the traffic lights to change.

The replacement bus service on Coventry Road was well established by this time using Metro-Cammell-bodied Daimler CVD6 vehicles. On its way out of the city on a 60 route working to Cranes Park Estate is 1986 (HOV 986), one of 28 of the class allocated to Coventry Road garage. *Birmingham Public Works Department*

**Below** Once across the Sandy Lane junction, Coventry Road began to climb up Kingston Hill. MCCW-bodied Leyland six-wheeler 34 (OC 1134) waits at the bottom of the hill at the Bordesley Park Road stop, before moving away towards the Sandy Lane junction. The disused Stechford tram lines, abandoned on 2 October 1948, remain in silent testament to a mode of transport that had recently been closed. To the right of the trolleybus is Bordesley Park Road, along which ran the Bolton Road 22 tram service, abandoned on 4 February 1930.

On the right the tall chimneys of the mid-1850s terraced housing look far from cared for, yet would survive for another 20 years. Opposite is the dark wall of J. & W. Mitchell's paper mill. Looking up the hill, there is an area of open space that would have been used for dualling this section of road if the war had not intervened. At the top of the Kingston Hill, behind the trolleybus, is Coventry Road depot. *R. Wilson*

Looking in the opposite direction we get a better view of J. & W. Mitchell's large Victorian paper mill, which dominated this section of road. The mill would survive into the 1970s, when the site, after many years of dereliction, would become part of the Middle Ring Road.

The passing of one generation of vehicles and the beginning of another is shown here. The 1934-built Leyland TTBD2 trolleybus is 34 (OC 1134), and is working on the 94 route to Sheldon. It has only a few months left in service before its withdrawal. Behind it is 2141 (JOJ 141), a Leyland 'Titan' PD2/1 with a Leyland body built in 1949, which would see service until November 1967. It is running on one of Hockley garage's cross-city turns to the Whittington Oval in Yardley. *S. N. J. White*

## In and around Coventry Road depot

Leyland TTBD2 trolleybus 23 (OC 1123) with a Metro-Cammell body, pulls away from the stop outside Coventry Road (Arthur Street) depot on a 94 service. This impressive building received its first trolleybuses when the service to Yardley was converted from trams on 7 January 1934. With its almost ecclesiastical windows, it depot dominates the top of Kingston Hill rather in the way that a large church might have done!

The trolleybus is about to pass a rather splendid 1948 Jaguar Mark V, while behind is almost new Crossley-bodied Crossley DD42/7 2458 (JOJ 458), which had entered service in June 1950, working into the city on a 15B service. Although there is a 16-year interval between the construction of the two vehicles, the continuity of the Birmingham City Transport bodywork 'house style' is noticeable. The livery of the two vehicles is basically the same, while the typical BCT characteristics begun in 1929 had been refined over 25 years to produce a uniquely Birmingham look. *Courtesy of Travel West Midlands*

A photograph not to be resisted was this one taken outside the closed Coventry Road garage in July 1996! Nearly half a century after the previous photograph, the preserved ex-BCT Crossley 2489 (JOJ 489) now represents the old order, as it recreates the trolleybus operation by displaying an original 94 trolleybus destination blind. Behind it is one of the newest double-deckers owned by West Midland Buses, 3243 (H243 LOM), a Scania N113DRB with an Alexander H45/31F body, which entered service in November 1990. It is working on the appropriately numbered 57 route, which almost duplicates the former 96 trolleybus route, going from High Street to Solihull via Coventry Road and Lode Lane. *D. R. Harvey*

Waiting for a driver change outside the depot is 78 (COX 78), the last of the 1937-built, MCCW-bodied Leyland TB5s, working on the 94 service to Albert Street. It had been given a 'light touch-up and varnish' in October 1950, which was the equivalent of a repaint! Its black-painted front mud-guards can be distinguished from the dark blue of the lower panels. Although the design of the body was in many ways rather conservative, the concealed trolley gantries and the distinctive mouldings and livery produced the impression of a thoroughly up-to-date, if somewhat idiosyncratically styled vehicle. *R. Marshall*

Climbing Kingston Hill over the abandoned Stechford tram tracks and the cobbles of Coventry Road and about to turn right into the depot is 1940-built Leyland TB7 88 (FOK 88). A number of the bus garages had their own destination display, but the Coventry Road trolleybus fleet had to be content with the anonymous 'DEPOT ONLY'. These FOK-registered trolleybuses represented the last style of pre-war Birmingham-style bus body. They perpetuated the long front wings that had been introduced on the COX-registered trolleys, which by 1940 were a little old-fashioned.

Following the Morris Ten-Four car down the hill is Walker Brothers' post-war Austin 10hp van, with its streamlined wings; Dinky Toys made a model of this type of van in the early 1950s. Following the trolleybus is a wartime Ford V8 utility estate car running on oversized military-style tyres. *T. Barker*

One of the garage mechanics man-handles a bamboo pole to try to put the wayward negative trolleypole of Leyland TB7 four-wheeler 85 (FOK 85) back on to the overhead wire. The vehicle had been working on the 94 route into the city, but had suffered some major problem as the rear emergency exit had been opened so that the garage staff could gain access to the poles.

It is Saturday 30 June 1951, the last day of operation, as suggested by the abandonment notices in the windows. It is possible that this failure might have been 85's last, as it is broken down outside the depot! *L. W. Perkins*

Kingston Hill's steep quarter-mile climb from Bordesley Park Road reaches the Cattell Road junction at the Greenway Arms, which can be seen behind the distant six-wheel trolleybus. Standing outside Coventry Road depot is Leyland TB5 68 (COX 68), working on a 92 service from Yardley. Behind MCCW-bodied Daimler COG5 123 (EOG 123), which is travelling out of the city, are the Victorian-built shops that lined Coventry Road opposite the depot.

Beyond the Greenway Arms junction, along Cattell Road, is the St Andrew's football ground of Birmingham City. On match days the 84 tram route to the city terminus via Deritend was supplemented by trolleybus extras, which usually showed 'FOOTBALL SPECIAL' in their destination blinds. *T. Barker*

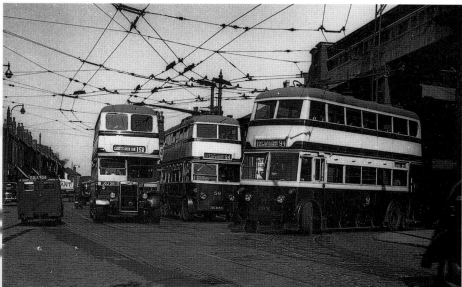

Leyland TB5 trolleybus 71 (COX 71) emerges from the dark depot entrance into the bright summer sunshine of 1950 prior to taking up a duty on the 94 service. It is negotiating the complicated overhead wiring arrangement that allowed access to the depot as well as normal service running, and pulls out due to the courtesy of the driver of the Leyland six-wheeler, 59 (OC 1159). Alternatively, the more cynical view is that the driver of 59 is letting out the four-wheeler so that he doesn't have to carry so many passengers, thereby making his next trip easier!

One of Liverpool Street garage's exposed-radiator Crossley DD42/7s, 2281 (JOJ 281), is working into the city on a 15B service from Garretts Green Lane. This bus had the dubious distinction of being one of the first of its class to be taken out of stock after being involved in an accident in December 1963, which caused severe damage to the platform. *W. A. Camwell*

On a quieter occasion, Metro-Cammell-bodied Leyland TTBD2 trolleybus 58 (OC 1158) reverses into the depot with the aid of a member of the garage staff, who is standing on the platform giving reversing directions to the driver while holding on to the black 'Doverite' plastic-covered stanchion. This covering was employed so that passengers would not get an electric shock when they boarded the metal-framed trolleybus. It is to be hoped that the driver understands the usually vague arm signals of the garage mechanic!

The curving tram tracks into Coventry Road depot as well as those in Coventry Road and Cattell Road, to the left of the Greenway Arms in the background, were made redundant when the Stechford tram route was abandoned on 2 October 1948. The tracks were eventually pulled up some years after the closure of the trolleybus system. *W. A. Camwell*

**Top** With its paintwork glistening in the afternoon sun, Leyland TB7 82 (FOK 82), one of the 1940 batch of trolleybuses, turns into the gloom of Coventry Road depot in the last few weeks of trolleybus operation. The wartime 28hp Bedford OW lorry with its civilian-style cab mated to the military-style sloping bonnet, has swung out to overtake the turning trolleybus as it descends Kingston Hill on its way towards Bordesley.

The Metro-Cammell trolleybus body of 1940 had all the improvements that were introduced with the 1938 deliveries of Daimler COG5s and Leyland 'Titan' TD6cs. These included the larger rear upper saloon emergency exit windows and the similarly enlarged rear platform window. *R. T. Wilson*

**Middle** In order to accommodate the trolleybuses in the tram depot, a second entrance gate was made. Leyland TTBD2 32 (OC 1132) stands at the original entrance with the fan of tram tracks leading out into the main road. Outside the offices on the left are parked a number of trolleybuses, the rear one being 63 (OC 1163).

Coventry Road depot had been opened on 24 November 1906 and became fully operational as a tram depot a few weeks later, early in 1907. Between the closure of the Bolton Road 22 tram route on Tuesday 4 February 1930 and immediately before the replacement of the Coventry Road trams on 7 January 1934, it was partially rebuilt from total tram operation to contain the new fleet of 50 trolleybuses as well as the 40-plus trams required for the two Stechford services.

The modern Leyland six-wheelers radically altered the speed and frequency of the service on Coventry Road. The juxtaposition of these latest vehicles sharing the depot with open-balconied, four-wheeled trams seemed something of a contradiction! *J. S. Webb*

**Bottom** The anachronism of the Stechford route was that the outer part of the route was the last tramway extension to be opened in Birmingham, on Tuesday 26 August 1928, and was on a central reservation. By contrast, the tramcars were open-balconied, four-wheelers built in 1912. The 301 Class trams, such as car 385, had replaced the ex-Radial 71 Class cars after April 1939, but they had only been expected to run on the route for about another year as the intention had been to abandon the Stechford routes.

In this 1948 view, the year in which the Stechford tram route closed, the modern-looking trolleybuses look as though they have a long future in front of them. The following year, the intended sequence of the last tram route closures was announced and the Coventry Road trolleybuses were surprisingly included in this scheme to wipe out electric traction in the city.

The trolleybus next to the tram is Leyland 78 (COX 78), which at this time was only 11 years old. On the extreme right is 25 (OC 1125), while in the background are two trolleybuses with their roofs and rear domes still painted in wartime khaki. *J. S. Webb*

*Top* After the abandonment of the Stechford trams, Coventry Road garage acquired a large fleet of new Daimler CVD6s from the 1756-1843 Class. In addition a number of pre-war Daimler COG5s were drafted in from other garages, and here 1196 (FOF 196), a 1939 MCCW-bodied example, stands alongside 1937 Leyland TB5 71 (COX 71), near the entrance to the garage in 1951. No 1196 was withdrawn in 1954 and eventually saw service in Cyprus, cut down to a single-decker!

The 1937 delivery of trolleybuses had bodies that were very similar to the design that was placed on the BOP-, COX-, COH- and CVP-registered Daimler COG5s. The EOG- and FOF-registered buses of 1938 and 1939 were a slightly more up-to-date version of the earlier style. It was this basic design that was fitted to the 1940 FOK-registered trolleys. They had the dubious distinction of having the last pre-war BCT-style bodies to be constructed. All Birmingham trolleybuses from number 17 had bodies built by MCCW, which rather went against the bus body buying policy, which was to dual-source its purchases with the Birmingham Railway Carriage & Wagon Company of Smethwick getting about one-third of the orders and eventually supplying some 245 bus bodies. *F. Lloyd*

*Middle* The last day of operation was captured by a number of photographers, but none more poignantly than this one! On any other day the departure from Coventry Road garage by a trolleybus would have been of little interest. What makes this special, as Leyland TTBD2 32 (OC 1132) waits for its driver at the garage entrance before taking up its duties on the 'main-line' 94 service, is that lurking in the background are the brand new diesel-engined buses that would take over on the following day. *C. Brown*

*Bottom* A rather dusty 57 (OC 1157) turns out of the depot on the last day of operation. This Saturday was just like any other, with trolleybuses humming up and down Coventry Road, their trolleywheels hissing on the overhead, every 2 or 3 minutes. It was only the notices of the impending abandonment in their windows that revealed the inevitable outcome at the end of the day. Standing just inside the garage entrance, awaiting its fate in the scrapyard of W. T. Bird, is the already withdrawn 17 (OC 1117), which would be towed away later that same Saturday afternoon. *J. Hughes*

*Left* The administration offices of Coventry Road garage were on the eastern side of the premises, and 1940-delivered Leyland TB7 85 (FOK 85) stands alongside them on 16 June 1951. On entering the garage the trolleybuses would be driven around the perimeter wiring to the rear of the premises, where they could be parked beneath any three of the four sets of wiring on roads 16 to 19. The remaining parking facilities were in the first six roads adjacent to the exit; this meant that all the trolleybuses leaving the garage had to do a hard left turn to gain access to Coventry Road.

The trolleybus displays the simpler, unlined post-war livery style and the large unshaded fleet numbers; unusually for such an early date, the seating capacity, usually displayed below the rear registration plate, has been omitted. *R. Wilson*

*Below* The tram service along Coventry Road was closed on the evening of Saturday 6 January 1934 and the new fleet of 50 Metro-Cammell-bodied Leyland TTBD2 six-wheelers entered service the following morning. Here Nos 41, 42 and 47 are lined up next to the depot entrance on roads 1, 2 and 3, immediately before entering service.

The delivery of these trolleybuses began in November 1933 and the last did not enter service until March 1934. They were tested over the Nechells route before being stored in Perry Barr bus garage; they were then towed to Coventry Road just before the service started. *M. R. Keeley collection*

*Right* Viewed from the first floor offices of the garage is trolleybus 59, (OC 1159). This unusual angle shows the externally framed gantry arrangement to support the trolleypoles on the six-wheeler. All the later four-wheelers had their roof pillars internally braced to support the weight of the polework, which gave them an uninterrupted roof profile. The wooden duckboarding on the roofs of the two trolleybuses was used to gain access to the overhead; that on the newer four-wheeler, 90 (FOK 90), is supporting a mechanic. Each of the trolleybuses carries a pair of what look like upside-down dustbins on their roofs; these are radio suppressors.

The trolleybus driver in these Leyland TTBD2s had a spacious cab in which to work, with the electrical contractor panel to his left and the circuit breakers usually mounted on the cab ceiling. Driving this 8 ton 17 cwt 3 qr trolleybus was rather like driving a heavy electric milk-float, except that it was limited by the overhead wiring. A fully laden trolleybus was quite difficult to drive as it involved applying power and very carefully observing the position of the vehicle in relation to the overhead.

Despite these restrictions, trolleybus operation had certain advantages: it was a method of public transport that was cheap to operate and maintain; before nationalisation it frequently used electricity produced locally; it provided the public with a fast and reliable service and gave the operator a good vehicle life expectancy in relation to the initial capital outlay. The 50 OC-registered trolleybuses of 1934 cost Birmingham Corporation some £95,000; spreading that over their 17 years of service, each vehicle effectively cost only £111 per annum! *R. A. Mills*

*Below left* The interior of Coventry Road depot was re-surfaced after the Stechford trams had been taken off, but the trolleybuses used the first six roads for parking and gradually wore through the asphalt, revealing the tram tracks once again. On Sunday 3 June 1951, among some 20 parked trolleybuses, two Leyland TB5s, 73 (left) and 67 (middle) are at the front of roads 5 and 6; the COX-registered trolleybuses are identifiable by the upper saloon rain strip above the front windows. On the extreme right is trolleybus 85 (FOK 85), which was one of the 1940 batch of Leyland TB7s; these were built without the front rain strip, which gave them a more modern appearance. The TB7s could also be easily identified as they were the only BCT trolleybuses equipped with trafficators, which were mounted above the front wheel arch on the cream moulding below the cab side window. With only one month to go before the system closed, the condition of the vehicles remained smart, although repaints had finished in the previous November. *D. R. Harvey collection*

*Below right* The Coventry Road fleet remained intact until February 1951, when Leyland six-wheelers 24, 39 and 51 were taken out of service and stored. Between then and the final closure on 30 June 1951, two more trolleybuses were withdrawn, while in the last weeks of operation a number of others were removed from service. Parked next to the entrance of the garage, they were towed away for scrap on the final day of operation by the scrap merchant W. T. Bird to the famous Stratford-on-Avon graveyard of withdrawn buses.

These three dusty vehicles had obviously been taken out of service some days before. Four-wheeled Leyland TB5 68 (COX 68) and Leyland TTBD2 17 (OC 1117), in company with another of the six-wheelers, have had their destination blinds removed and their fleet numbers, civic crests and legal ownership painted out. This was normal BCT practice when a vehicle was withdrawn, although it certainly did not conceal the identity of the individual vehicles. *L. W. Perkins*

**Top** Later the same afternoon the No 68 was taken out of Coventry Road garage behind one of Bird's ex-RAF 4x4 AEC 'Matador' 0853s for the 23-mile tow to Stratford. Over 9,000 of these lorries were built, and at the end of the Second World War a large number were put up for sale. Along with many other contractors, hauliers and HGV operators, Bird's found that these fairly new four-wheel-drive lorries were extremely useful towing vehicles. The normal Saturday service continued while the initial clearances were made; one of the 17-66 batch can be seen working on its way into the city. *L. W. Perkins*

**Middle** Coventry Road depot/garage was also known as Arthur Street, which was the name of the side street that ran beside the western side of the premises. The street's grim 19th-century three-storeyed terraces stand in a state of terminal decay as another of Bird's AEC 'Matadors' prepares to tow six-wheeler 50 (OC 1150) to the scrapyard.

This rigid tow was undertaken by Bird's who were responsible for clearing the whole fleet of 74 trolleybuses between the Saturday afternoon of 30 June 1951 and the evening of 1 July. Thirteen of them were taken to Cunliffe's yard in Wellington Road, Handsworth, for storage, as Bird's could not manage to tow all the fleet to Stratford in the allotted time. The trip to Stratford was a colossal task, as each lorry had to undertake a round trip of nearly 50 miles. At least six lorries were used; with a top towing speed of only about 20 mph, there was an almost continuous shuttle between Coventry Road garage and the scrapyard throughout that weekend.

Behind the trolleybus is the open yard of the garage, which served as an extra parking area for the bus fleet. The rear of one of the 1948 Metro-Cammell-bodied Daimler CVD6s from the 1756-1843 Class can just be seen there. *L. W. Perkins*

**Bottom** Two trolleybuses are parked in Arthur Street behind their towing lorries on Saturday 30 June 1951 before being taken to Bird's scrapyard. The distant four-wheeler is Leyland TB7 79 (FOK 79), which would languish for at least six months while abortive attempts were made to sell it and the rest of the FOK-registered class of trolleybuses. It was rumoured that the class of 12 vehicles was to be sold to a buyer in South Africa, but the deal fell through and they, like the rest of the trolleybus fleet, were broken up by the end of 1952.

The six-wheeler is 19 (OC 1119), which had been one of the five TTBD2 vehicles temporarily withdrawn and stored throughout October and November 1940 as surplus to service requirements after the closure of the Nechells route. On this Saturday afternoon, however, it was the real thing, and 19 had run the last of its 507,000 miles of revenue service! Trolleybuses were towed away with their motors almost still warm as the contract with Bird's stipulated that by Monday 2 July the garage would be cleared of trolleybuses. *L. W. Perkins*

BIRMINGHAM TROLLEYBUSES 1922-51

*Above* On a wet January morning in 1934, Leyland TTBD2 six-wheeler 35 (OC 1135), working on a 93 service to Station Street, is posed for the photographer just short of the depot entrance with the Greenway Arms in the background. As it is only a few days after the introduction of the service there has not been time to remove the old tram stop which displays the legend ALL CARS STOP HERE.

To the left of the trolleybus is Cattell Road, which took the 84 tram route to Bordesley Green, extended to Stechford only five years earlier. Today, although the road layout remains roughly the same, all the buildings in the background have been demolished. The land in Cattell Road is part of Birmingham City's St Andrew's car park, while the land on which the pub and the row of shops stood awaits development as part of the Birmingham Heartlands Project. *Courtesy of Travel West Midlands*

## Small Heath to Yardley

*Above right* A wartime Guy 'Arab' II, 1408 (FOP 408), which entered service on 13 June 1944, fitted with an MoWT-style Park Royal body, comes out of Cattell Road beneath the tram wires of the Stechford route. It is working on a driver-training duty and will raucously bark its way over the cobbles to join the main Coventry Road in front of the Greenway Arms. Drivers taught on these buses, with their unforgiving 'back-to-front' gearboxes, could literally drive anything!

The trolleybus overhead at this point had an interesting addition, which was also found at other junctions along the A45. Just below the eaves of the Greenway Arms and next to the negative wire on the out of town overhead was a line of electric light bulbs, which guided the trolleybus drivers around the unmarked bend during foggy conditions. In the days of winter industrial smogs, which frequently reduced visibility to a few feet, these lights were a real advantage for the drivers as they inched their way along the route. *D. R. Harvey collection*

Leyland TTBD2 trolleybus 21 (OC 1121), one of the 50 Metro-Cammell-bodied 58-seater six-wheelers, takes the turn in front of the Greenway Arms along Coventry Road towards Small Heath in 1950. It has just passed Coventry Road garage, whose entrance was opposite Miss Hilda Collins's canvas-canopied coffee shop. The building on the right is Bastocks funeral directors, housed in premises that somehow survived the wartime bombing that destroyed the shops on either side. The square building in the background is the Kingston cinema, opened on 4 August 1935 with a seating capacity of 1,475. *F. Lloyd*

The view in July 1996 in front of the site of the Greenway Arms bears little resemblance to the earlier one To the left of preserved Crossley 2489 (JOJ 489) is the rectangular block of what used to be the Kingston cinema, which was closed on 14 December 1968 and converted to a bingo hall, but has stood boarded up and derelict since late 1996. The junction with Herbert Road, on the east side of Coventry Road garage and behind the Ford Escort saloon, has been closed off in a 'traffic calming' scheme. Everything else from 1950 has been demolished. The gates on the right lead to the wide open spaces of the car park at the front of Birmingham City's football ground; for many years the whole of the football ground was surrounded by terraced housing dating from the 1860s. Seen through the summer heat haze on the right is the Rotunda standing at the top of the Bull Ring, about 1½ miles away in the city centre. *D. R. Harvey*

The crowd of waiting city-bound passengers invade the rear platform of six-wheeler 20 (OC 1120) at Regent Park Road outside Turner's corn merchants. The trolleybus stop attached to the traction pole was the typical hexagonal style that was unique to the BCT trolleybus system.

No 20 is working on the 94 service through this inner part of Small Heath. The shops dated from between the 1870s to the turn of the century; this was the first suburban shopping centre on the route after Digbeth. Opposite the loading Leyland, two doors away from Jay's furniture store, is a Wimbush's bread and cake shop. A. D. Wimbush's nearby bakery in Green Lane is today still very much part of the Small Heath scene, as it is the headquarters of the 'Three Cooks' organisation.

The smell of freshly baked bread has permeated this part of the city for many years. Wimbush's Bakery was founded in 1904 by Ambrose Durant Wimbush in Small Heath, and became one of the largest bakeries in the Birmingham area, moving to its present premises in 1913. In 1956 it was taken over

by the Ranks-Hovis-McDougal group, and today owns some 145 retail outlets and supplies over 1,000 other shops with bread and cakes. *A. Yates*

The lights suspended to aid trolleybus drivers in the fog were also in place at the Green Lane junction, which Leyland trolleybus 37 (OC 1137) has just passed in 1950. It is following another member of the class, 32 (OC 1132), which is working on a 99 route short working to Wagon Lane.

On the extreme right the group of people are waiting to catch the next city-bound trolleybus. To the left, on the gable-end of one the buildings in Green Lane, is an advertisement for Barbers Teas, which were blended and packaged in Pershore Street. *W. A. Camwell*

Only isolated pockets of Coventry Road have remained unaltered since the demise of the trolleybuses in 1951. One of these areas is just beyond the Green Lane junction, where the double frontage of the Curtess shoe shop was occupied in 1951 by Freeman, Hardy & Willis, one of the best known shoe retailers in the country. Beyond Curtess's shop is an older three-storeyed Victorian terrace. Such buildings as these are becoming quite rare in the city, but this row has survived and has been modernised, although one chimney stack has been lost in the intervening years.

Looking towards the distant Golden Hillock Road, some of the old buildings remain in this part of Small Heath. Even the advertising hoarding remains on the corner of Green Lane, although in the summer of 1996 it carried just one large advertisement for Marlboro cigarettes. *D. R. Harvey*

On its way out of the city is Metro-Cammell-bodied 58-seater 54 (OC 1154), parked between Green Lane and Grange Road outside the Brighton Arms public house. Ironically, next door to the pub was a Methodist Chapel! Above the Chestoyle Cars sign on the skyline is the tower of Small Heath public library in Green Lane.

No 54's paintwork looks in good condition, having been overhauled only a few months earlier in May 1949. During their service lives these trolleybuses remained largely unaltered, even to the extent of retaining the rather old-fashioned dividing rubbing-strip on the lower saloon side panels. One feature that was removed was the off-side destination box over the two small staircase windows; this fell into disuse about 1941 to save the wear on linen and was never re-introduced after the war. *C. Carter*

**Top** Once beyond Green Lane, Coventry Road widened out and was flanked by 19th-century premises that had been built as houses, but had been converted to shops before the First World War. The shuttered frontage of L. G. Mills's greengrocers suggests that this view of Leyland TB7 82 (FOK 82) was taken on a Sunday. In those early post-war days, all shops stayed shut on the Sabbath, which perhaps accounts for the lack of pedestrians. The trolleybus is working on a 94 service and has just passed Whitmore Road on its way into the city.

The single-storeyed shops to the rear of the trolleybus were built in the 1920s, and in 1949 the row was occupied by a hairdressers, the Princess Pat Cafe and Maturi Brothers, the cutters, whose vans roamed the streets of Birmingham sharpening the knives of butchers, grocers and householders, and still occupy the same premises today. In later years this part of Coventry Road developed into an area of car showrooms, but for now the trolleybus, running through 'half-deserted streets' (T. S. Eliot), reigned supreme. *R. Marshall*

**Middle** When Birmingham opened the new Coventry Road trolleybus service in January 1934, it created one of the most intensive services in the country with, in theory at least, a trolleybus every 2 minutes. This photograph shows that the theory was wrong! An almost new Leyland TTBD2, 38 (OC 1138), working on a 92 service from Albert Street, leads two other members of the same class through Small Heath on their way to Yardley. Passing the Golden Hillock Road junction is a trolleybus working on a 93 service to Station Street. In front of it is one of the AEC 'Regents' bodied by Brush in 1929 from the 338-367 batch, which is about to pass on its offside the junction with Muntz Street. The houses on the corner of Golden Hillock Road would have been about 70 years old at this time. In later years many large terraces along main roads out of the city such as these would be converted into shops, often struggling into post-war years before giving up their residential status. *J. Whybrow collection*

**Bottom** Standing at the stop outside Barclays Bank on the corner of Golden Hillock Road is Metro-Cammell-bodied Leyland TTBD2 32 (OC 1132), picking up passengers on its way into the city on a 94 service in 1949. The Victorian dwellings still display architectural embellishments such as the arched entrance, with pilaster columns, over the doorways. This style fell out of favour in the 1880s as an unnecessary expense when speculative Victorian entrepreneurs built houses to a more austere style. *F. Lloyd*

*Top* The handbrake, according to instructors, was 'the trolleybus driver's friend', being used to aid smooth starts, alter automatic frogs (though not in Birmingham), pull the trolleybus up to a halt and help to manoeuvre smoothly in traffic. The driver of six-wheeled Leyland TTBD2 61 (OC 1161) of 1934 has his hand on the handbrake in preparation for a smooth pull-away from the Golden Hillock Road stop outside the myopic sign of Harrison's Opticians. The slightly tarnished state of the paintwork would suggest that the trolleybus is in its second year of service. It is on the 92 route to Albert Street, which is displayed in the lower saloon offside destination box. *S. Eades*

*Middle* The City of Birmingham Tramways steam tram depot served the route along Coventry Road, which was opened on 16 January 1886 and terminated opposite Small Heath Park. The original terminus was at Dora Road, but this was cut back after 18 months of operation to the reversing triangle that gave access to the steam tram depot.

Small Heath Park had been opened on 5 April 1878 on a 44-acre site given to Birmingham Corporation by Miss Louisa Ann Ryland. It was visited by Queen Victoria on 23 March 1887 and was for many years known as Victoria Park. On the other side of the park was the terminus of the 22 Bolton Road route, seen on page 10 of Volume 2 of *A Nostalgic Look at Birmingham Trams*. By the 1930s the park had become a lung of greenery among the late-Victorian villas and terraces in the area.

Leyland TTBD2 trolleybus 53 (OC 1153) passes the low wall of the park on its way out of the city on the 94 service. It is standing at the stop facing down the hill in Coventry Road just beyond Charles Road and the former site of the steam tram yard. The cyclist is passing the Co-operative store, while the trolleybus stands adjacent to the canopied Douro wine store. *F. Lloyd*

*Bottom* One of the rarer workings along Coventry Road was the 99 service, and Leyland six-wheeler 58 (OC 1158) leads three other trolleybuses while on this short working to Wagon Lane. It was a rush-hour service, introduced on 24 January 1949, which utilised the new loop just beyond the Wagon & Horses public house, the last turn-back in Sheldon before the Arden Oak terminus about a mile away.

The Inspector is talking to the trolleybus driver at the stop at the entrance to the Hay Mills turning circle, which was particularly useful for the workers' specials from the Singer car works, which is the large 1930s building behind the traction pole on the left. Singer had first gone into production in 1905 and had a reputation for making rather staid cars with a myriad of variations. In the 1930s the company produced a real winner with the two-seater Le Mans, but failed to capitalise on its success because of lack of finance. By the mid-1950s sales of the Hunter range were disappointing, and the Singer car factory was closed on 18 August 1953, when it was producing the SM1500. The company was taken over by the Rootes Group by 1956, but this proved the 'kiss of death' for a number of famous British marques such as Hillman, Humber and Sunbeam, as nine years later the combine became part of the Chrysler Corporation; in 1970 the name Singer was dropped after a series of 'badge-engineered' cars based on existing Hillman models. On the extreme left is the Eatonways coach garage, and parked in its forecourt is one of their Burlingham full-fronted Leyland 'Tiger' PS1 coaches. *T. Barker*

The tree-lined loop at Hay Mills was used in the first weeks of the Coventry Road trolleybus route to photograph the new fleet, including in January 1934 brand new Metro-Cammell-bodied Leyland six-wheeler 19 (OC 1119). When new, these trolleybuses had chrome-covered front hub-caps, which generally only lasted until the first overhaul; what did remain were the slightly old-fashioned glass rain-louvres over the lower-saloon opening windows. On the roof, just in front of the trolley gear, is one of the pair of radio suppressors, as earlier trolleybuses had a disastrous effect on radio reception. It appears that Leylands 18 and 19 were used for the official Birmingham Corporation trolleybus photographs. The first member of the class, 17 (OC 1117), after its early completion and demonstration around the Old Square in the autumn of 1933, was painted in fleet livery after the rest of the class following its brief outing in its grey livery, and would not enter service until 25 March 1934. *Ribble Enthusiasts Club*

The turning circle at Hay Mills was located on the out-of-city side of the route just short of the Plough & Harrow public house at the gates of Heybarnes Park and Recreation Ground, an area of parkland occupying both sides of the River Cole. The Cole valley was prone to flooding at this point and as a consequence the surrounding land was never developed. The park acted as a divide between the Victorian growth in Small Heath to the west and the former Urban District of Yardley to the east.

Posed in the turning circle in 1940 is Metro-Cammell-bodied Leyland TB5 67 (COX 67), which looks very smart after being painted in the full wartime livery while in Kyotts Lake Road for an overhaul in November 1939. As well as the grey camouflaged roof and the headlight masks, the mud wings, the front skirt and the life-rails have been painted white. Even the driver's step has been given this treatment! *Courtesy of Travel West Midlands*

The turning circle was generally used only at peak periods by the trolleybuses, and the occasional 56 service to Hay Mills from Albert Street turned in the loop before returning to the city. The wooden fences (or palings as they were known in Birmingham) give an almost rural appearance to the loop as Leyland TTBD2 41 (OC 1141) waits before turning back towards Small Heath in April 1951. *T. Barker*

Seen in 1951 is Metro-Cammell-bodied Leyland TTBD2 49 (OC 1149). With the trees in the Hay Mills loop in full leaf, this vehicle is seen very close to the final closure date. It had been overhauled on 21 January 1949 and after 18 months in service the cream paintwork is beginning to look a little shabby. *S. N. J. White*

Waiting adjacent to the loop is trolleybus 76 (COX 76). This 1937-built Leyland TB5 has just dropped off its passengers on its way out of the city on the 94 route to Sheldon.

The mother strides purposefully away from the trolleybus stop with her young daughter, who is wearing a fashionable ribbon-bowed headband. On this warm day in the summer of 1950 the trolleybus waits for the conductor to signal the driver to pull away; without trafficators they had to rely upon the driver's hand signals. The COX- and FOK-registered trolleybuses differed from the corresponding buses by having a full-length driver's door signalling window. *W. A. Camwell*

A dusty Leyland TB7 86 (FOK 86), one of the 12 Metro-Cammell 54-seaters, has stopped short of the hexagonal trolleybus stop outside the Hay Mills turning loop. On this warm spring day in 1951 the driver has his windscreen ajar. Behind the trolleybus is the small row of shops next to Haybarnes Recreation Park, parked in front of which can be glimpsed a typically large American saloon, which appears to be a 1937 Buick. *S. N. J. White*

**Top** On its way into the city on the ubiquitous 94 route is 78 (COX 78), the last of the 1937-built Leyland TB5s. Although it is 1949, the four-wheeled 53-seater trolleybus still has the pre-war style fleet numbers. It has dropped off passengers opposite the Hay Mills turning circle. Next to the entrance to the out-of-city turning circle are the display boards of Eatonways Coaches outside its booking office. *L. W. Perkins*

**Middle** The Hay Mills loop occupied only a small area just short of the River Cole bridge. Looking eastwards, beyond the trees on the left lies the Heybarnes Recreation Ground, while the first building beyond the river bridge is the Plough & Harrow public house. This Ansell-owned pub had been built in the late 1890s and incorporated a curious turret on one corner. Beyond this, the serried ranks of steeply gabled shops give way to a more austere style of two-storeyed premises.

This flat valley crossing point on Coventry Road soon gave way to the steep climb up to Yardley. The tall building on the skyline above the Commer van is the Adelphi cinema, which opened on 10 October 1927 and closed on 31 August 1968 with a showing of *Blue*, starring Terence Stamp. The author's own memory of this cinema is seeing Elvis Presley in *Blue Hawaii* about 1962 accompanied by a herd of mice marching up and down between the rows of seats!

In this 1950 view Leyland six-wheeler 32 (OC 1132) stands behind an unidentified four-wheeler. Noticeable is the excellent state of the overhead, being taut and well strung and showing little sign of the sagging between the traction poles that afflicted many other systems. *W. A. Camwell*

**Bottom** The wide A45 of 1950 has today given way to an eight-lane dual carriageway, at the expense of all the buildings on the south side of the road. The Plough & Harrow with its turret still remains, as does the row of shops going towards Yardley. The buildings on the right were all demolished in 1984, including the Hay Mills Tavern, which stood alongside the River Cole about where the large tree stands in the middle of the photograph and the Hay Mills Congregational Church, which was built in 1899 at the corner of Kings Road.

Behind the barriers on the left is the now cut-off turning circle, one of the few features peculiar to the trolleybus system in Birmingham that has survived to the present day. The palings and the trees have all gone, although the Cole valley is still used as playing fields and a public open space. *D. R. Harvey*

BIRMINGHAM TROLLEYBUSES 1922-51

Sunday 1 July 1951 saw the first diesel-engined buses working normal all-day services along Coventry Road, although buses had been employed on the hourly NS94A night service since the introduction of such services on all the city's main roads on 15 April 1946. Underneath the de-energised trolleybus wires, Daimler CVD6 2629 (JOJ 629) has climbed the hill in South Yardley and has arrived at the Swan stop at Church Road. Behind the bus the three-storeyed houses have been converted to other uses, such as a dentist's surgery, a motoring school and, on the corner of Willard Road, a doctor's surgery. In the distance, beyond the gap in the buildings, are six shops, and there was inter-war housing all the way to Hay Mills Police Station at Holder Road. *R. W. Routh*

Looking towards the Swan terminus from Hay Mills, a Brill top-covered tram, still with flop-over destination boards, stands at the top of the hill outside South Yardley Police Station just before the First World War; today the police station is the Old Bill & Bull public house. The horse and carriage stand outside the grocers shop with a lot of its produce stacked outside on trestles near the Flora Road junction. The row of shops beyond Flora Road were the last ones before reaching the Swan shopping centre.

Views on this part of Coventry Road are most uncommon and there is no known photograph of a trolleybus on this uphill stretch of Coventry Road. This photograph does show, however, the wider road and slightly less built-up nature of the area. *Commercial photograph*

## Around The Swan, Yardley

Four Leyland six-wheel trolleybuses are at the compulsory stop at Yardley or rolling up to it in 1950. Nos 55, 21 and 56 are all working on the 94 service to the city boundary. This midday view shows the high frequency operated along the route. The rear trolleybus, 55 (OC 1155), stands opposite the exit from the Yardley trolleybus station.

Behind the traction pole with the roundabout sign on it is one of George Harris's drapery shops; this one sold children's and men's clothes and occupied the two shops at 1486 and 1488 Coventry Road, while a third shop at 1500 Coventry Road was the ladies-wear department; this was the penultimate retail outlet before the Church Road junction. Shops like this have largely disappeared because they cannot compete with the multi-national stores in the middle of Birmingham and out-of-town shopping centres. *W. A. Camwell*

**Top** The announcement in 1949 of the abandonment of the Coventry Road trolleybus route at the end of June 1951 came as something of a shock: the service would close before the Bristol Road and Erdington group of tram routes were abandoned, with 24 of the trolleybuses being less than 14 years old. This compared rather better than some of the tramcars working on these last routes, which in some cases dated from before the First World War!

At Kyotts Lake Road Works, where the trams shared the overhaul facilities with the relatively small trolleybus fleet, the overhauling and repainting of trolleybuses was gradually wound down. Metro-Cammell-bodied Leyland TB7 85 (FOK 85) was one of the last trolleys to receive 'a light touch up and varnish'(!) at the end of May 1950, and is seen here on Saturday 3 June near the Yardley terminus, having climbed the hill from Hay Mills. The immaculate 85 is showing the anonymous DEPOT ONLY destination display on the blind, having arrived empty from the depot. In front of the four-wheeler is Leyland TTBD2 32 (OC 1132), on its way to the city boundary at Sheldon, at the stop outside George Davies's saddlery shop, whose canvas canopy is lowered. *J. H. Meredith*

**Middle** Metro-Cammell-bodied Leyland TTBD2 46 (OC 1146) stands at the out-of-city stop near to Church Road in June 1951; the abandonment notices are in the windows of the trolleybus and the replacement bus stop post has been put in place next to the traction pole with the trolleybus stop. A long queue of people hoping to travel towards Sheldon wait as the last of the disembarking passengers leave the already rather full trolleybus.

No 46 has been overtaken by a 1933 Singer 14/6, while coming round the Swan island from Yardley Road is an early post-war Austin 10, following a Morris 8 convertible dating from about 1935. *R. Wilson*

**Bottom** The Swan underpass scheme, built between 1965 and 1967, has completely swept away all the old landmarks, and carries the A45 from the city centre towards Birmingham International Airport, the National Exhibition Centre and Coventry. Despite being up to four lanes wide, it still cannot cope with the demands of present-day traffic. Crossley 2489 (JOJ 489) stands at approximately the same position as trolleybus 46. Beyond the bus the multi-storey Tivoli Centre guards the entrance into Church Road, which, although only a few yards from the concrete rebuilding of the 1960s, remains virtually unaltered since the demise of the trolleybuses. The shopping centre was named after the Tivoli cinema, opened on 17 October 1927 and closed on 1 July 1961 with a showing of *The Facts of Life* starring Bob Hope and Lucille Ball. *Sarah J. Harvey*

Empty trolleybus 80 (FOK 80) pulls away from the setting-down stop at Yardley and is about to go round the Swan island and turn into the trolleybus 'station'. It is making this manoeuvre as it is working on the 92 route short working to Yardley from Albert Street. On page 13 of Volume 1 of *A Nostalgic Look at Birmingham Trams* tramcar 86, working on the 15 route, can be seen at roughly the same place in 1933. *J. S. Webb*

The Standard Flying 14 saloon speeds towards the Church Road junction as Leyland six-wheeler 42 (OC 1142) moves past Arthur Hemmings's building contractor's yard, having just left the Yardley stop on its way out of the city.

The method of collecting the 550 dc current from the overhead on Birmingham's trolleybuses was by trolley wheels. On most British trolleybus systems these were replaced by carbon inserts on the trolley heads, but for Birmingham pedestrians an approaching trolleybus could always be heard well in advance by the 'swishing' noise of the trolleywheels on the overhead. *R. Wilson*

The couple running for the trolleybus, the man holding a well-wrapped-up child in his arms, perhaps think that the almost new trolleybus is about to leave the Yardley terminus. Had they gone around to the front they would have seen that the driver's cab was empty!

Leyland TTBD2 trolleybus 26 (OC 1126) waits in the cold March sunshine one Sunday morning in 1934 before returning to Albert Street on a 92 service. Parked outside Tonks the baker and confectioner, facing towards the Church Road junction, is an equally new Standard Ten. Sidney Tonks at No 1498 Coventry Road, George Davies the saddler next door, Henry Lake the haulier, and Arthur Hemmings the building contractor at No 1490 were all still trading when the trolleybuses were abandoned 17 years later. *J. Whybrow collection*

Seen at the Yardley terminal loop opposite the Swan public house and adjacent to Yardley Road is almost new Leyland TTBD2 47 (OC 1147). It is Wednesday 5 September 1934 and the Coventry Road trolleybus service to Yardley has been operating for some nine months, long enough for any operating or vehicle problems to be ironed out. The paintwork on the Metro-Cammell body clearly shows the black-painted front wings and the gold lined-out lower blue panels. This vehicle is working to the Albert Street terminus on the 92 route, which had taken over from the 15 tram service. The little girl on the extreme right, wearing a wide-brimmed hat, and the men near to the ornamental street lights on the left wearing slacks and a jacket add a real 'period' feel to the scene. *F. Lloyd*

The conductor of trolleybus 28 (OC 1128) takes his break standing next to his charge. He is carrying a Bell Punch ticket-rack and leather money satchel and is probably curious why anyone would want to photograph such a mundane thing as a trolleybus at night! The six-wheeler is parked at the Yardley terminus in about 1938 and is working on a 93 service to Station Street. This night photograph also reveals some of the detail of the vehicle that would otherwise not be seen, including the wooden fittings in the upper saloon and the extra blue lining-out above and below the between-decks blue-bands. *S. Eades*

The 'sylvan glade' of the Yardley loop actually consisted of two trees! This terminus was used by all the trolleybus services on their way into the city including the Lode Lane and Sheldon services as well as the Yardley short workings. Trolleybus 53 (OC 1153) stands in the turning loop before leaving for the city, about 4 miles away, on a 94 service in 1950.

To the rear of the trolleybus is the site of the former City of Birmingham Tramways Yardley depot, which had been closed in about 1913 when the Corporation decided that it was surplus to requirements. R. H. Collier took over the site and it became the firm's car showrooms, known locally as Collier's Corner. During the Depression Colliers built Clyno cars in 1929 and Swifts in 1931 from bankrupt stock parts. *W. J. Wyse*

*Right* The driver of trolleybus 55 (OC 1155) leans nonchalantly against his vehicle at the Yardley trolleybus terminus, as a Midland Red GHA-registered Daimler CWA6, recently rebuilt by Willowbrook, negotiates the Swan island on its way into the city. This island was at the junction of Coventry Road with Yardley Road and Church Road, and was part of the city's Ring Road between Acocks Green and Stechford. During 1926 it became the well-known Outer Circle, 11, bus route, whose 25-mile journey circled the city.

The two elderly men in gabardine coats and caps are sitting on the bench next to the red telephone box. This timeless design has only recently been phased out and replaced by state-of-the-art, vandal-proof kiosks that offer neither privacy nor protection from inclement weather! *W. J. Wyse*

*Below* The palindromic numbers of the two trolleybuses at the Yardley trolleybus loop also show the refinements in trolleybus design between 1934 and 1937. Leyland TB5 72 (COX 72) has turned into the stop next to the green-painted wooden shelters. It is working on the 'main-line' 94 service from Sheldon and has passed the parked Leyland six-wheeler 27 (OC 1127); empty of both passengers and crew, it will also return to the same Albert Street city terminus as 72. The loop was wired up for such overtaking manoeuvres, so that the short working trolleybuses on the 92 and 93 services could turn back to join the apparently never-ending series of trolleybuses working on the 94, 95 and 97 services into the city. *W. J. Wyse*

On a warm sunny afternoon in late summer 1950, trolleybus 27 (OC 1127) is seen again, this time on the through line of the overhead at the Yardley loop while employed on the 94 service. It is in front of an unidentified COX-registered MCCW-bodied Leyland TB5 working back to Coventry Road depot. The driver of the six-wheeler looks across to the packed four-wheeler 78 (COX 78), whose driver has just moved to the offside of his vehicle to turn the key in the Bundy clock before working on the 93 service to Station Street. *W. A. Camwell*

The most common destination blind displays on the Coventry Road trolleybus services were the 93, 94 and 97 routes. Usually a trolleybus running back to the depot would display DEPOT ONLY. It was very unusual for a trolleybus to display the 98 blind, as this was only applicable on a 94 service short working from the city boundary at the Arden Oak at Sheldon to the Cattell Road junction, about 100 yards short of the depot entrance.

Leyland six-wheeler 59 (OC 1159) shows the 98 display and is parked in the Yardley turning loop on the overhead used for lay-overs and turn-backs. Leyland TB7 87 (FOK 87), full of passengers, waits for its driver who is climbing into his cab via the nearside door. Birmingham trolleybuses built after 1932 were unusual as they had nearside as well as offside cab doors. *W. A. Camwell*

In preparation for the trolleybus abandonment, the Bundy clock at Yardley was moved from the middle of the traffic island to the more conventional position on the pavement adjacent to the bus stop. The hexagonal trolleybus stop has been removed and the bare pole of the bus stop, on the extreme right, can be seen waiting for the replacement 'To-City-Stage' bus stop to be fitted.

The trolleybus driver waits to 'peg the clock' before climbing through the cab and resuming his journey on the 94 route to Albert Street. He is about to drive MCCW 54-seater Leyland TB7 83 (FOK 83). When disposed of to Bird's of Stratford for possible resale, this trolleybus, along with 90 (FOK 90), was sold to Silcox of Pembroke Dock, who mounted the body on a new Bristol K6G chassis and registered this strange combination as ODE 402. The bodies on 83 and 90 were chosen by Silcox because of their good condition, noticeable in this mid-June 1951 view. This vehicle was the only one of the class to be fitted with a non-standard traction motor ventilation grille below the registration number. *M. Rooum*

*Top* The FOK-registered Leyland trolley-buses entered service in February 1940 and were nominally replacements for the 1931 Leyland TBD1 half-cabs used on the Nechells service. They were destined to have only 11 years of service life in a fleet operating on Coventry Road that had an average life of just over 15 years. No 79 (FOK 79) negotiates the Swan island on its way into the city on the 94 route. It is being followed by a very early post-war square-fronted Ford Anglia and a later almost new example with the modern sloping front. Passing the 1930s shopping block on the corner of Church Road and Coventry Road, which included Lloyds Bank, is a Standard Flying Fourteen. To the right, behind the cyclist, is the 'modern' wing of The Swan public house. *J. H. Meredith*

*Middle* Leyland TTBD2 trolleybus 60 (OC 1160) passes in front of The Swan Hotel in 1951 on its way into the city on the 94 route; it is crossing the Yardley Road junction before turning into the old tram turning loop. From the early years of this century until 1920 a regular open market was held adjacent to the site of the tram loop opposite the Swan Hotel. Behind the trolleybus is a Standard Flying Nine two-door saloon, dating from just before the war.

This was the second Swan hostelry on this site, having replaced a much rebuilt 17th-century coaching inn about 1899. The original Swan Inn was located on the site of the car park in front of the pub entrance. This Victorian mock-Tudor building was itself replaced in 1964 by a third Swan, which claimed to have the longest bar in Britain and be the largest pub in Europe! It proved, however, to be a soulless white elephant that was totally out of character with the drinking habits of the area, and was deservedly closed in the 1980s to be replaced by an office block! *F. Lloyd*

*Bottom* The road sign destinations to Coventry and Northampton via the A45 would seem somehow irrelevant and distant to most of the trolleybus passengers. This was an age when the public relied on public transport and when the average 'man in the street' rarely ventured beyond the limits of the local bus service. A tram or, as in this case, a trolleybus route would be seen as limiting even more the accessibility of places beyond the city boundary.

On Sunday 6 February 1949 GEC-powered Leyland TTBD2 21 (OC 1121) swings around the island at The Swan working into the city on a 94 service. The man on the platform is getting ready to jump off, an art that has been lost by the travelling public since rear-entrance open-platformed buses disappeared from the streets. This skill is, however, kept alive in London, on routes that still operate AEC 'Routemasters'! Behind the 'tree' of road signs is Church Road, which leads to the Yew Tree junction, while to the rear of the trolleybus, outside Albert's carpet shop, is a horse-drawn milk-float making local deliveries. *G. F. Douglas*

*Above* Having let the Standard Vanguard Phase I estate car pass, the driver of trolleybus 59 (OC 1159) now has to wait for the 1947 Vauxhall Twelve-Four to negotiate the complicated junction outside The Swan public house. It was necessary to have a double island for traffic using the Outer Ring Road as the Vauxhall car is doing. The trolleybuses were able to use the first island when turning back to the city on a 92 or 93 service, and the single line of overhead between the two nearest traction poles was used by trolleybuses going into the 'station' at Collier's Corner on these two short workings.

Remnants of wartime blackout road markings are still in evidence, most prominently on the substantial road sign, directing to all points east with a splendidly vague set of destinations. In the mid-1930s block of flats next to Lloyds Bank was Harding's bakery shop; Hardings Royal Steam Bakery was based in Yardley and, as well as having six retail outlets on the eastern side of the city, also delivered bread door-to-door using battery electric vans. *W. A. Camwell*

*Below* Looking back to the Yardley trolleybus station from the forecourt of The Swan Hotel, this view shows the large area covered by the loop. The almost self-supporting island had on it a shelter, toilet facilities, resting places, a clock, modern means of communication and a frequent means of transport to escape from it! On Wednesday 30 May 1951 the only thing missing from this almost Plomley-esque idyll was anywhere to obtain sustenance and somewhere to buy a gramophone and eight records!

Of the four trolleybuses in this view, only the rear one in the loop is a four-wheeler, being one of the 1940-built FOK batch of Leyland TB7s. Of the three Leyland six-wheelers, only 50 (OC 1150), coming out of the city on the 94 route, can be identified. About to turn behind it is a Morris-Commercial CV-type 2-ton van owned by the Birmingham Co-Operative Society.

Today all this is a memory, swept away when the Swan underpass was built, leaving the hub of South Yardley as a cutting through which to pass on the way to the National Exhibition Centre, Birmingham International Airport and Coventry. *G. F. Douglas*

# Out to Sheldon

*Right* On Wednesday 30 May 1951 Leyland TB5 76 (COX 76) leaves the Yardley island on a 94 service towards Sheldon. In the penultimate month of trolleybus operation this vehicle ran a total of 2,881 miles, making it one of the hardest worked vehicles of its class. Behind the cyclist following the trolleybus is, rather unusually for this date, an imported Fiat 500. This type was known as the 'Topolino' and was one of the first really successful 'mini' cars, with 498,384 being produced between 1936 and 1948.

The imposing corner block of late Victorian shops included Robinson's chemist shop; a chemist had occupied these premises since the early years of the century, when it had been known as the Yardley Pharmacy. At that time it stood opposite an old 18th-century farm building that survived until the 1930s as the premises of a painter and decorator. The Standard Flying Fourteen car is parked where this old farm outhouse used to stand. *G. F. Douglas*

*Below* Until the early 1960s the area around the Swan island remained essentially a small suburban shopping centre, and it was only with the opening of the A45(M) beyond Coventry leading to the M1 motorway to London in 1958 that the increasing traffic congestion along Coventry Road made it necessary to widen the road and convert it into a dual carriageway. All the buildings east of the Swan island were demolished to make way for the Swan underpass. The buildings on the left of this photograph were replaced in 1962 by the ill-starred Tivoli shopping centre, one of the first suburban, pedestrianised shopping areas in the city, but it was marooned on three sides as it was only accessible by pedestrian underpasses. The first in the row of seven gabled Victorian shops on the right of the trolleybus is the premises of the Birmingham Co-Operative Society, and between there and Charles Edward Road is a hairdresser, boot repairer, sweet shop, wet-fish merchant and grocer. Behind the second traction pole on the right is the half-timbered New Inn, which was more of a 'local' than the nearby Swan.

Metro-Cammell-bodied Leyland TTBD2 66 (OC 1166) was delivered in March 1934, but only ran 68 miles before actually entering revenue service in June of that year. It accelerates across the Belisha crossing, with its trolley wheels swishing on the overhead as it goes on its way to the city boundary. The black and white 'zebra' road stripes at Belisha crossings were not introduced until later in 1951, after the trolleybuses had gone. *R. Wilson*

**Top** The crowd of intending passengers at the Midland Red stop on the left spill into the road as they look for the next bus to take them to Sheldon or Coventry. Although Coventry Road was the main eastern route out of the city, in 1951 the number of private cars using it was, like everywhere else at that time, quite small. Of the four that are visible, the one about to overtake the trolleybus is an early post-war Morris Eight saloon, followed by an Austin 10 saloon.

The man looking into Fawcett's ironmongers shop would hardly recognise the Do It All-type of superstore that would consign shops like these to a distant memory, occasionally remembered by an evocative smell, such as Jeyes Fluid or carbolic soap. Next door in the six-gabled block is the Retone shop, which, with a name like that, could only have been a dry cleaner!

Leyland TTBD2 trolleybus 35 (OC 1135) is about to leave the Charles Edward Road stop working into South Yardley from Sheldon on the 94 route. Behind it in the next block is the mock-Elizabethan frontage of the New Inn. This Butlers Brewery pub advertises on its sign that it has 'Pleasant Gardens'; these lay to the rear of the premises along with a bowling green, and are almost forgotten adjuncts to the social life of this small pub. *R. Wilson*

**Middle** The brick building beyond Charles Edward Road is the modern New Inn, which replaced the older one in 1983 after a period of over 15 years when the pub used a temporary prefabricated structure. All the old premises on the north side of the road were swept away as part of the Coventry Road dual carriageway scheme, while those on the left in the previous photograph stood in line with the present-day central reservation. *D. R. Harvey*

**Bottom** After coming out of the cafe in Coventry Road, near Gilbertstone Avenue, the conductor will have put the crew's billy-can of tea into the cab to be consumed in a few minutes time when they reach the Arden Oak terminus. Metro-Cammell-bodied Leyland TTBD2 29 (OC 1129) is working on the 94 service in the last year of operation.

Today, this section of Coventry Road is unrecognisable; it is now a three-lane dual carriageway that took over most of the grass verges that so characterised this section of road in the 1950s. Another fairly recent change to the area was the demolition of the austere 1930s-styled Good Companions public house, replaced by Harry Ramsden's rather splendid fish and chip restaurant in 1994. *R. Wilson*

*Top* When the trolleybuses were extended beyond Yardley on 5 July 1936, they were passing through parts of Lyndon End and Sheldon that had not yet been built on and were still rural agricultural areas, although increasingly threatened by the ever encroaching city. Sheldon had only become part of the city in 1931, as Birmingham could offer the area better-quality public utilities and services.

Still painted in its original lined-out livery is Leyland TTBD2 20 (OC 1120), travelling towards Yardley on a 94 service on Thursday 22 April 1937. The lorry travelling out of the city is a canvas-tilt-bodied Leyland 'Retriever'. No 20's trolley booms are extended to the offside as the inward overhead wiring was offset near to the out-of-city line. *D. R. Harvey collection*

*Middle* On its way to Yardley in New Coventry Road is trolleybus 58 (OC 1158), working on the 94 route. The New Coventry Road had been opened before the extension of the trolleybus route to Sheldon to relieve congestion on the original road through Lyndon End. Behind the Ford Y-type van and to the left of the 'Sold to Jack Cotton' sign is the old road.

The climb from Lyndon End to the top of New Coventry Road at Brays Road gave the trolleybuses the opportunity to use their 65hp GEC traction motors to the full; stiff climbs made very little difference to their performance. *J. S. Webb*

*Bottom* The dispersal of trolleybuses away from Coventry Road depot at night between 1941 and 1942 usually involved parking them facing towards the city in New Coventry Road with their trolleypoles pulled down. As many as 40 could be parked here if an air raid was thought to be likely. This part of the city was well away from Coventry Road depot and the heavily industrialised area of Small Heath, which was part of the inner city that attracted enemy bombers.

Two Leyland TTBD2s, 21 (OC 1121) and 50 (OC 1150), stand parked in New Coventry Road between Wagon Lane and Brays Road, wearing the full wartime livery modifications that were necessary because of the black-out regulations. Both are carrying advertisements, with the leading vehicle extolling the virtues of economy rather than financial thrift.

New Coventry Road was something of an operating oddity as it appears that powers were never sought to construct or run trolleybuses on this new stretch of road. It seems that rather than operate in the original section of Coventry Road against the flow of traffic, the Transport Department decided to consider the whole project as 'road widening', which was allowed under the terms of the Birmingham Corporation Act of 1922, which enabled BCT to directly replace any tram route with trolleybuses. It also circumvented the need for new Parliamentary approval to erect wiring and operate the trolleybuses on New Coventry Road as it was considered to be a 'diversion' from the original route. *R. Wilson*

*Top* The housing beyond Steyning Road and the Good Companions public house had developed on open land during the late 1920s and throughout the 1930s. These large semi-detached houses in Coventry Road, with their bay windows and mock-Elizabethan frontages, would have cost about £395 when new. They proliferated in the outer suburbs throughout the city, and represented the new inter-war housing standards at affordable prices in the private market. The prime site on the corner of Coventry Road and New Coventry Road had, by 1951, been sold to the Birmingham property entrepreneur Jack Cotton, but it remained vacant for many years before a petrol station was built there in the late 1950s.

Leyland six-wheeler 64 (OC 1164) slows down at the Brays Road stop to allow the alighting passenger to 'drop off' in the traditional manner. Brays Road took its name from a Doctor of Divinity, Thomas Bray, who was rector of Sheldon in 1690 and founded the Society for Promoting Christian Knowledge. *R. Wilson*

*Middle* Lyndon End, which trolleybus 60 (OC 1160) is approaching, consisted of a collection of Georgian and Victorian cottages clustered around the Wagon Lane-Barrows Lane junction. The latter had been the original route into the medieval village of Yardley from the Coventry and Meriden direction.

The trolleybus, which appears to be carrying a full complement of passengers, travels down the hill towards the large Wagon & Horses pub, which replaced an earlier hostelry of the same name in the late 1920s. The rows of nine-barred telegraph poles dominate the street furniture on this part of Coventry Road and even make the traction poles and trolleybus overhead appear insignificant. *R. Wilson*

*Bottom* When the bus-operated night service NS94A was introduced on 15 April 1946, the Wagon & Horses public house at Lyndon End was its terminus. There was also the facility for trolleybuses to turn short and return to the city via New Coventry Road; the turn-back was used for the first time on 24 January 1949 and was the last new piece of trolleybus wiring to be erected on the system. To the right is the Rondelle petrol filling station, which was situated at the eastern apex of Coventry Road and New Coventry Road. One of the 17-66 Class uses the new wiring while 62 (OC 1162) and an unidentified Leyland TB5 wait to continue along Coventry Road towards Sheldon. When No 62 was withdrawn it and 14 other trolleybuses were sent to Cunliffe's of Handsworth, where they were stored in a yard in Wellington Road until mid-1952, when all 15 were taken to Bird's to join the rest of the doomed fleet. An early post-war Hillman Minx saloon is overtaking in this spring 1951 view. *R. Wilson*

*Above* Following a schoolboy on a bicycle and having just overtaken a Humber Hawk car, 33 (OC 1133) accelerates past a similar six-wheeler, 62 (OC 1162), which is turning back to the city at the Rondelle garage on a 99 short working. The turn-back into New Coventry Road was sufficiently tight that the overhead wires had to have an extra loop so that the turn could be more easily negotiated. No 33 is coming into the city on the rarely used 96 service from the Rover Works in Lode Lane to Albert Street; most of the Rover services went to Station Street as 97s. The hoarding in the background advertises Phillips' Grand Cut tobacco, a blend of Virginia tobacco that for many years was one of the best-selling pipe-tobaccos in this country. *W. A. Camwell*

*Right* Tired-looking Metro-Cammell-bodied six-wheeled Leyland TTBD2 34 (OC 1134), with a fully laden lower saloon, accelerates into New Coventry Road at the Rondelle garage, working on the 94 service to Albert Street. This superb photograph, taken by the late Arthur Camwell,

reveals a lot of detail about these vehicles. Even at this late stage of their careers, the lower saloon opening windows still have their glass rain louvres intact; in many fleets these would have probably been replaced with aluminium ones or simply removed, but that was not the way things were done in Birmingham!

These trolleybuses had nearside cab doors, whose purpose was really superfluous, but unlike the later four-wheelers they at least did not have nearside cab door signalling windows (presumably for drivers with long left arms!). The upper saloon design

seemed more modern than the lower saloon, although the radio interference suppressors on the front of the untidy crab-claw-like supports for the trolley gantry rather clutter up the roof area. Another feature not usually visible from outside is the small vertical handrail behind the central front window pillar. This style of Metro-Cammell body lacked the moulded lower saloon cream band and moulded blue bands. This perhaps detracted from the appearance of these impressive vehicles, especially in later days when, as in this case, they began to look a little old-fashioned and a little care-worn. *W. A. Camwell*

The driver of trolleybus 42 (OC 1142) negotiates the overhead junction at the bottom of New Coventry Road while working into the city on the 94 route. Nearly empty, it pulls away from the row of shops opposite the Rondelle garage. Leaving the garage forecourt, next to the Bass sign for the Wagon & Horses public house, is an Austin KB8 Three-Way van, which is the only other vehicle on the road.

Through the trees can be seen the bollards that marked the junction of Wagon Lane and New Coventry Road. Wagon Lane marked the boundary between Birmingham and Solihull UDC, and for many years the residents of this part of Solihull could only get to Birmingham by using the trolleybus service, necessitating a long walk from the large 1930s housing estates. *R. Wilson*

Leyland TTBD2 six-wheeler 62 (OC 1162) speeds past the Lyndon End turn-back on its way out of the city on the 94 route. It has just overtaken the motorcycle combination whose sidecar appears to have had a puncture, while opposite the Wagon & Horses pub is a 1938 Morris Eight Series II saloon. The turn-back loop on the overhead for the 99 service crosses into New Coventry Road in front of the Rondelle garage. *J. S. Webb*

Coventry Road at Lyndon End, on the outward part of the former trolleybus service, was further developed in the 1980s, such as Sheldon Court on the left. The Wagon & Horses pub, whose sign can be seen on the left, and the petrol station, although by now an Elf garage, still occupy the bottom of the hill in Coventry Road. Opposite is Lyndon End Recreation Ground.

The most noticeable difference between 1951 and 1996, when ex-BCT Crossley 2489 (JOJ 489) is seen at the same spot, is just how cluttered the sky-line was in the earlier view! Despite the trolleybus overhead and the proliferation of traction and telegraph poles, there were only two street lights on the 1951 view! This was then considered adequate, and in fact the trolleybuses only ran with their headlights switched on at night in Lode Lane! *D. R. Harvey*

Having negotiated the overhead junction at Lyndon End, the driver of Leyland six-wheeler 34 (OC 1134) is faced with the prospect of his billy-can of tea getting cold before he can reach the Sheldon terminus! In front of him and inevitably going to slow him up is one of the AEC 'Mercury' tower wagons whose crew are doing some work at a span wire. Such work was normally done in the dead of night and overhead repairs during the day were most uncommon. In the distance, coming into the city, is another of the 17-66 Class, but in this case it still has a wartime grey-painted roof. *West Midland Buses*

The Coronation bunting still decorates the Co-operative shop's frontage in June 1953, almost two years after the passing of the 'Silent Service'. One of the replacement Daimler CVD6s, 2655 (JOJ 655), wearing smart wheel trims, stands near the junction with Sheaf Lane working on the 58 route; behind is an exposed-radiator HOV-registered Daimler CVD6. During the Coronation week Birmingham's buses carried two small flags in a two-holed bracket mounted below the destination blind; this can be seen on 2655 just below the letters 'NT' in the word 'COVENTRY'. *D. R. Harvey collection*

Sunday 17 June 1951 was the occasion of the LRTL's farewell trolleybus tour. Birmingham's last trolleybus, 90 (FOK 90), was used for the occasion, and is seen on its way out of the city at the Wheatsheaf junction with the less than common SPECIAL on the destination blind. The four-wheeler is following six-wheeled trolleybus 20 (OC 1120), working on the 94 route to the city boundary; the latter has just cleared the overhead junction, opposite Sheaf Lane, which will take the tour vehicle into the Lode Lane branch. About to overtake trolleybus 90 is a pre-war Ford Eight. Behind is a row of retail premises that includes the Birmingham Co-operative shop, as well as a Woolworth's store and a Barclays Bank. *J. H. Meredith*

Leyland TTBD2 34 (OC 1134) stands at The Wheatsheaf public house just beyond the Hobs Moat Road junction. This pub dated from the 1920s and replaced an earlier inn of the same name. On the forecourt, parked outside the 'Outdoor' - that almost forgotten aspect of the public house - is an Austin Three-Way van. These were an early post-war forward-control 25 cwt commercial, the equivalent to the ubiquitous Ford Transit vans of today; their globular styling was reminiscent of the Austin Somersets of the same period. In front of the van is a Morris Ten-Four two-seater, which is about 18 years old. The right-hand curve of wiring took the 96 and 97 routes into Hobs Moat Road and on to the Rover works at Lode Lane. *R. Wilson*

The man with the push bike crossing the road in 1951 is doing what in the 1990s would be almost suicidal across an eight-lane carriageway! Coventry Road has been widened out of all recognition, with overhead traffic-light gantries. This junction is reputably the busiest in suburban Birmingham.

This part of Sheldon has totally lost its original 1930s look and the whole area has been rebuilt with anonymous 1970s shop and office blocks. The frontage of the pub has remained largely unaltered, although it is now a hotel with a large extension to the rear; this was built in order to exploit the recently developed business from the National Exhibition Centre. *D. R. Harvey*

Four-wheeled Leyland TB7 81 (FOK 81) has just loaded up its last passenger before moving off on a city-bound 94 service. It is standing outside the forecourt of The Wheatsheaf public house next to the hopelessly inadequate tubular steel bus shelter. Behind it the sweep of Coventry Road disappears into the distance towards the boundary at Tiger's Island where the top deck of the next inbound 94 service trolleybus is just visible. This section of Coventry Road, with its late inter-war housing, had the distinction of having the highest numbered house in the country, reaching 2589 at the city boundary!

Prominent in the row of shops to the left is a George Mason grocery shop, while the shop next door with the white awning is a branch of J. H. Dewhurst, the Birmingham-based butcher that in 1950 had 34 retail outlets in the city. To the left of the trolleybus in the same row of shops was Shakespeare's newsagent and tobacconist shop, which appears to have had the monopoly of paper deliveries in the area, as they also had a shop on the opposite corner in Hobs Moat Road. *W. A. Camwell*

**Above** Fully-laden trolleybus 79 (FOK 79), the first of the 1940 batch of Leyland TB7s, waits in Hobs Moat Road for six-wheeler 54 (OC 1154), working into the city on a 94 service, to come into The Wheatsheaf stop after crossing the overhead pointwork. The 94 service was regarded as being the 'main-line' working and it was normal practice for the Lode Lane services to wait. To the left of the six-wheeler, next to the out-of-city overhead, is another row of festoon lights to help trolleybus drivers leaving Hobs Moat Lane to judge their position in foggy weather. Views of trolleybuses at this junction are very rare, but W. A. Camwell photographed this scene one sunny afternoon in the summer of 1950 when standing next to the rather splendid wooden pub sign. *W. A. Camwell*

## Arden Oak terminus

**Below** Beyond The Wheatsheaf junction, the late-1930s houses stretched towards the city boundary. In later years this type of urban growth was frowned upon by town planners as it wasted valuable land in and around what was later to become the 'green belt'. In the 1930s land speculation along main roads captured ribbon-like strips of land; it was only later, around 1936, that fill-in developments were built, such as the nearby Cranes Park Estate, which lay to the north of the radial Coventry Road.

The articulated Commer Superpoise lorry, belonging to the newly nationalised British Road Services, slogs its way out of the city as Leyland trolleybus 36 (OC 1136) starts on its 7 mile 1,221 yard journey on the 94 route into the city. The wide verges and the trees disappeared when the road was widened to cope with amounts of traffic that would have been unheard of in the 1950s. *H. Harcourt*

*Above* A group of mothers with their children stand with their prams, undisturbed by the lack of traffic on the main A45 road looking towards the trolleybus terminus at Arden Oak Road. Even in 1949, when this photograph was taken, Sheldon was at the very edge of suburbia. The distant line of trolleybuses is waiting in Coventry Road before turning into the terminus loop as Leyland TTBD2 43 (OC 1143) starts back towards the city on another 94 service to Albert Street. *Courtesy of West Midlands Buses*

*Below* Having arrived and unloaded at the Sheldon terminus, trolleybuses waited in Coventry Road to gain access to the turning circle and loading stop at Arden Oak Road. Metro-Cammell-bodied 58-seater Leyland TTBD2 23 (OC 1123) stands near the setting-down stop; it is empty and the crew might have walked to the nearby tea-bar caravan, which was usually parked at the terminus. Before leaving his trolleybus, the driver will have switched off the circuit breakers that isolated the electric power coming in from the overhead to the traction motors, enabling it to be parked with its trolleypoles on the wires. Trolleybuses, like battery-powered milk-floats, had three gears, forward, neutral and reverse; 23's driver should have put his vehicle into neutral before leaving the cab.

Birmingham's six-wheelers had two methods of being operated: by overhead and by skate and positive overhead. The COX- and FOK-registered four-wheelers had the added facility of a third method, which was means of traction batteries. The GEC WT25 65hp motors were mounted amidships beneath the lower saloon, enabling the cab area to be reasonably uncluttered, which had certain operational advantages for the driver.

At the rear of the trolleybus the platform stanchions were covered with black Doverite instead of the chrome used on the contemporary diesel-engined buses; this prevented passengers from getting an electric shock if they were standing on the pavement and also in contact with the stanchion. *D. R. Harvey collection*

Leading this line of seven trolleybuses is one of the ubiquitous six-wheelers, in this case 46 (OC 1146). Having unloaded their passengers, the trolleybuses waited to move into the Arden Oak Road turning circle, which is off the photograph on the right. No 46's driver has just pulled away from the front of the line and has put on a touch of right lock so that he can manoeuvre his trolleybus more easily into the turning loop. The first three vehicles and the last two are members of the six-wheeled 17-66 Class, while the fourth is one of the FOK-registered batch of four-wheelers and the fifth one of the 1937 batch of COX-registered vehicles.

This view was taken in 1950, although everything else dates from before the war. The semi-detached houses date from the late 1930s, as do the two cars, an Austin Ten and a Morris 8 two-door convertible. *D. W. K. Jones*

In November 1950 Leyland TTBD2 60 (OC 1160) waits at the unloading stop at the Arden Oak terminus in company with another member of the class. The destination blind shows the usual display of 'COVENTRY ROAD (CITY BOUNDARY) & ALBERT STREET' on three lines beside a large number 94, which, after 14 years, is beginning to look a little grubby. The roof also looks in need of a repaint, as this trolleybus was last given a 'touch-up and varnish' on 30 November 1948 at Kyotts Lake Road Works. *W. J. Wyse*

Leyland TTBD2 36 (OC 1136) is parked in the loop at Arden Oak Road, with its nearside cab door open, while its driver waits for his allotted departure time before turning the key in the Bundy clock to peg the time-tape. Another of the 17-66 Class waits at the unloading stop on the main road and will move into the loop as soon as No 36 has moved away. The 1930s streamlined caravan, parked on the grass verge, was a regular source of cups of tea for the crews at the end of their long journey from the city centre. *R. F. Mack*

This wartime view of the Sheldon terminus shows four-wheeler 73 (COX 73) parked at the entrance to the loop. In front of it, parked at the Bundy clock, is six-wheeler 42 (OC 1142), still painted in the fully lined-out pre-war livery, which helps to date the photograph to before June 1945, which was when the Leyland TTBD2 lost its lined-out livery.

As well as the usual wartime vehicle and road markings, there is an arrowed 'S' sign on the traction pole indicating where the nearest air raid shelter is situated. In these wartime days of petrol rationing, the couple on the tandem seem to epitomise the spirit of the period. *D. R. Harvey collection*

Another of the 17-66 Class, 32 (OC 1132), waits at the terminus turning circle to load up with some passengers before going back to Albert Street on a 94 service. In the background in Arden Oak Road are the late pre-war houses that had been built before the nearby Elmdon Airport was developed. In 1951 they were only exposed to the noise of twin-piston-engined aircraft, but today they are in the flight path of large passenger jet aircraft leaving and arriving at Birmingham International Airport. Even with the development of quiet multi-engined jets, double-glazing in these houses has become essential! *R. Marshall*

When the Omnibus Society undertook its tour of the system on 3 June 1951, the trolleybus that followed the tour vehicle to the city boundary was 38 (OC 1138). Despite its 17 years, the basic structure of the vehicle looks remarkably sound and there is no evidence of any body sag or any misaligned half-drop windows.

The driver of the 2.40 pm departure from the terminus looks inquiringly towards the enthusiasts standing around trolleybus 90, before getting into the cab through the nearside door and resuming his duty. *P. Yeomans*

**Above** The 1936 extension of the 94 route to Arden Oak Road added another 2.51 miles to the existing 5.23 miles of the route originally opened to Yardley. Leyland TTBD2 64 (OC 1164) is at the terminus in about 1950; it is empty and looks as if it will leave for Yardley with a fairly light load. This trolleybus amassed 534,052 miles in its service life, which was the fifth highest in the class, the highest mileage belonging to No 60, which ran 539,276 miles. *R. Knibbs*

**Below** The terminus at Arden Oak Road served the southern side of the Cranes Park Estate. Behind trolleybus 56 (OC 1156) is the small row of shops, typical of the type of retail outlets found throughout suburban Birmingham until replaced by supermarkets. Until the early 1960s this type of shopping area could support major retailers such as Wrenson's and Wimbush's.

The trolleybus terminus acted as a focal point for local public transport in the area. Most of city's route termini had a cluster of shops nearby and this developed into a symbiotic relationship. In this Sunday scene, a number of the shops, including Wrenson's, have their window blinds pulled down. *W. J. Wyse*

*Top* Photographic evidence and enthusiasts' recollections seem to suggest that the Lode Lane branch was worked by four-wheelers more than the higher-capacity six-wheelers. Similarly, the short workings to Yardley followed the same pattern, while the 'main line' to Sheldon was more likely to be worked by a six-wheeler.

Just to disprove the theory Leyland TB5 four-wheeler 76 (COX 76) stands at the terminus at Arden Oak Road in 1949. Behind the bushes on the right is Hatchford Brook, a tributary of the River Cole; until the late-1960s development of the huge Chelmsley Wood Estate, about 3 miles to the north, this stream had effectively marked the edge of the urban area to the east of the city. In 1949 there was still the feel that to ride on the trolleybus to the terminus was to go to the beginning of the countryside. *F. Lloyd*

*Middle* It is the summer of 1950 and the driver of Leyland TB7 83 (FOK 83) waits to peg the Bundy clock before climbing into the nearside cab door of his trolleybus. These FOK-registered 54-seater vehicles were fitted with traction batteries for off-wire manoeuvring. Despite the somewhat idiosyncratic BCT-styled bodies, which were modified versions of the contemporary bus bodies on Daimler COG5s and Leyland TD6cs, the mechanical specifications and passenger appointments for these trolleybuses were of a very high standard. The lower saloon had patterned moquette seats and side panels, while the upper saloon had leather-cloth-covered seats in the style of a gentleman's smoking room. With the standard straight staircase and roomy rear platform, only a glimpse into the fairly utilitarian cab spoiled the image of comfort! In the background, yet again, is the tea bar in the converted caravan. *D. Barlow*

*Bottom* The crew of Leyland six-wheeler 61 (OC 1161) wait to return to Albert Street, while in the background are some of the last pre-war detached houses to be built on the Coventry Road before the boundary was reached. It is a measure of how quiet the area was in 1951 that one of the occupiers to the right is able to cultivate his front garden!

The all-metal body style of these trolleybuses was sufficiently influential outside London that both the municipalities of Wolverhampton, on Sunbeam and Guy chassis, and Portsmouth, also on Sunbeam chassis, bought virtually identical 'off-the-peg' BCT-styled MCCW bodies. Even as late as 1935 Nottingham City Transport bought a batch of 30 Leyland TTBD4s whose Metro-Cammell bodies had their origins in the design of the Birmingham 17-66 Class. The Birmingham batch of 50 trolleybuses belonged to the 36th contract for metal-framed bodies built by Metro-Cammell, but OC 6567, the Sunbeam MS2 Commercial Motor Show demonstrator of 1933, and Wolverhampton's JW 4104 were the first two trolleybus bodies built by MCCW and had contract numbers of 24 and 25 respectively. *R. Wilson*

*Top* The trolleybus wires are still in place as Daimler CVD6 1816 (HOV 816) of 1948 stands in the terminus loop at Arden Oak Road. The bus carries notices announcing the replacement of the trolleybus services, but the new buses had the slightly less informative destination display 'SHELDON VIA COVENTRY ROAD' beside the number 58. The irony of the new services was that at Hobs Moat Road the replacement city-bound buses turned *left* into Sheaf Lane and on to the Cranes Park Estate, which had previously been served only by Midland Red. The former trolleybus route to the Rover Works which turned *right* into Hobs Moat Road had to be abandoned by the Corporation as it ran outside the city boundary and was still being operated under the original wartime emergency powers. Midland Red took over the service to the Rover works in Lode Lane with its X75 route that started outside St Martin's Church in the Bull Ring. *D. Griffiths*

*Middle* By 1996 Wrenson's grocery store and Wimbush's bread and cake shop have given way to less well-known owners, but the 1930s row of shops still retains the local service character. The various widening schemes over the years that have affected Coventry Road have altered the alignment of many of the entrances to the side roads, and the old trolleybus terminus has long since been swallowed up by Coventry Road's extra carriageways. The Arden Oak Road junction is now a simple T-junction, so it is impossible to reproduce the past scene exactly, but No 2489 (JOJ 489) stands as near as possible to the old trolleybus parking position on Sunday 21 July 1996 waiting to 'return to city' as a 94 route trolleybus. *D. R. Harvey*

*Bottom* The area to the north of the trolleybus turning circle was still rural, although about a mile away was the fairly new City of Birmingham airport at Elmdon, which had been ceremonially opened by HRH The Duchess of Kent on 8 July 1939 on a typical English summer's day - it poured with rain! The airport was closed after the outbreak of war and used for military purposes. Re-opened on 8 July 1946, its two grass landing strips could only take aircraft up to the size of Douglas DC3s and Vickers 'Vikings'. However, expansion of the airport was made possible by gradual growth into the surrounding land between the city boundary and Marston Green.

The driver of six-wheeled Leyland 42 (OC 1142) has pulled on a full right lock to turn his trolleybus out of the turning circle and on to the inbound wires of Coventry Road. A couple of minutes later, after moving up to the Bundy clock, the second trolleybus, 41 (OC 1141), will make the same manoeuvre. Beyond the turning trolleybus, beneath the willow trees, is a Midland Red Brush-bodied BMMO D5, built in 1950, which is working on the long inter-urban 159 route to Coventry via Meriden. *W. A. Camwell*

*Top* With the evening sun in the spring of 1951 casting long shadows, a mother sits on the bench with her young child in its pram by the trolleybus stop. GEC-powered 65hp Leyland TTBD2 34 (OC 1134) has almost completed the turn back into Coventry Road after leaving the terminus at Arden Oak Road. To the right of the trolleybus is a set of tied-off overhead wires; this 40-yard length of wiring was not connected to the turning circle, but it did have its own set of hangers, spacers and traction poles officially for electricity supply purposes. In reality these wires could have represented an abortive attempt to use the powers under the Birmingham Corporation Act of 1935, Part III, to reach the actual city boundary at Tiger's Island, some 0.4 miles beyond Arden Oak Road. Tiger's Island was a small islet in the middle of a lake, so was not the type of island that BCT engineers were looking for in order to turn their trolleybuses! The trolleybuses might even have reached Elmdon Airport had the Coventry Road route been further developed! *J. S. Webb*

The willow trees afford some useful shade to the waiting Midland Red passengers standing near the bridge over Hatchford Brook, just beyond the Belisha beacon. Trolleybus 60 (OC 1160) has just rattled its way around the overhead after leaving the Sheldon terminus of the 94 route, and the driver of the Midland Red D5, coming into the city, has let it out in front of him. Behind the approaching Bedford van is a Birmingham City Transport Leyland 'Tiger' PS2/1 single-decker working on the airport service to Elmdon. Introduced in 1949, this ran from Queens Drive, New Street station. *W. A. Camwell*

Parked opposite the Sheldon terminus loop at Arden Oak Road and facing into the city with its trolleybooms down and the bamboo pole propped against the back is once again No 90 (FOK 90), the Omnibus Society tour vehicle of 3 June 1951. In the loop is one of the 17-66 Class working on a 94 service. Once the trolleybooms have been put back on to the wire and the enthusiasts have re-boarded 90, it will execute the rarely made left turn on its traction batteries into Hobs Moat Road. Although the vehicle would do exactly the same three weeks later, on neither occasion does it appear to have been photographed for posterity! *A. Wakelin*

# The Lode Lane branch

*Top* Returning to The Wheatsheaf junction, an outbound Leyland six-wheeler, 42 (OC 1142), stands in Hobs Moat Road outside Shakespeare's newsagents shop. It is showing the fairly unusual destination display of 96, which had its city terminus in Albert Street; far more common was the 97 service, which terminated in Station Street.

The Lode Lane service was introduced on 29 October 1941 under the Emergency Powers (Defence) Parliamentary Act of 1939. The Ministry of War Transport approached Birmingham Corporation to suggest that a 1¼-mile branch be constructed along Hobs Moat Road and Lode Lane to the gates of the Rover car company's shadow factory built to produce aircraft engines. The Corporation did not have to seek Parliamentary Powers to operate trolleybuses on the route as the service was intended to provide transport for the wartime factory workers in this vital reserved occupation. The service was offered to BCT rather than Midland Red so that valuable fuel might be conserved. *W. A. Camwell*

*Middle* The distant shops on the corner of Sheaf Lane are the only remnants of the Coventry Road of 45 years earlier. The overhead traffic signs and gantry straddle the widened Coventry Road, while Hobs Moat Road has in turn been re-aligned and widened at the junction. On an extremely hot and sunny Sunday 21 July 1996 ex-BCT Crossley 2489 (JOJ 489) stands in the same place displaying 96 on the blind. The trees in Hobs Moat Road have all been cut down while Shakespeare's newsagents shop, with its mock wooden beams, has been replaced by an uninspired cubed-shaped office building. *D. R. Harvey*

*Bottom* The semi-rural nature of the wartime Lode Lane branch was quickly overtaken by the semi-detached housing developments that were completed in the early post-war years in Solihull. One thing that did not change was the intensive use made of the trolleybus service by the Rover car-workers. Leyland six-wheeler 25 (OC 1125), with the safety strap across the platform indicating that it is full, starts to negotiate the island at the Lode Lane end of Hobs Moat Road. It is following a Commer ice-cream van, which helps to date this view to the summer months of 1950. The trolleybus overhead disappears along Lode Lane towards the entrance to the Rover factory. The single-deck buses in Lode Lane were owned by independent operators who had works contracts with Rover. *W. A. Camwell*

*Top* Well-laden trolleybus 31 (OC 1131) swings out of the Rover works into Lode Lane in 1951, surrounded by cyclists and motorcyclists going home at the end of a shift. The Rover factory in Lode Lane was completed in late 1939 and by September 1940 was manufacturing Bristol Hercules aero-engines. After the cessation of hostilities, along with most British vehicle manufacturers, it resumed car-making, although for the first few years the cars that were built were little more than upgraded 1939-40 models, and the majority were built for export in a desperate attempt to bring much-needed money back into the nearly bankrupt British economy. New cars for the home market were restricted to a mere trickle until about 1948, which is the same year as the first new post-war Rover car, the largely forgotten P3 type. The real success story of Rover also came out in that year, which was a four-wheeled 'Jeep-like' utility vehicle christened Land-Rover. The rest is history! *W. A. Camwell*

*Middle* Lode Lane still retains the tree-lined status that it enjoyed when the trolleybuses went through Solihull UDC to the Rover car factory. The entrance road to the works is now controlled by traffic lights, but the comparison between the 1951 view and Crossley 2489 (JOJ 489) executing the same manoeuvre in 1996 reveals a marked similarity. The large ROVER CAR WORKS sign has gone, although the Crossley is masking an equally impressive one for LAND ROVER. *D. R. Harvey*

*Bottom* Leyland TB7 90 (FOK 90) has just negotiated the turning circle at the far end of the Rover service road and is accelerating past the area where parked, de-poled trolleybuses stood to wait at the loading stop; on the road can be seen the stains from the oil dropped on literally thousands of occasions when trolleybuses lay over at the terminus. No 90 is seen on Sunday 17 June 1951, and although it is displaying 96 on the destination blind it is in fact on an LRTL Tour. It is in excellent condition, and this was one of the reasons why it and 83 (FOK 83) were selected for further service by Silcox of Pembroke Dock, although unfortunately not as a trolleybus but a bus. The body was mounted on a Bristol K6G chassis and registered ODE 401, while the chassis was returned to W. T. Bird and scrapped along with all the other Birmingham trolleybuses. The body lasted until the summer of 1961 before being replaced. *A. D. Packer*

The trolleybuses turned left from Lode Lane into the private Rover service road before reaching a turning circle where they turned round before coming back to the loading point next to the factory buildings. Standing empty in a peaceful moment before the rush at the end of the shift is Leyland TB7 79 (FOK 79), waiting to return to Station Street in the city centre. These last BCT trolleybuses weighed 7 tons 10 cwt, which represented a 14 cwt increase over the corresponding Daimler COG5. Behind it is six-wheeler 20 (OC 1120), which is working on the 96 service to Albert Street. *W. A. Camwell*

Perhaps the most difficult photograph to recreate was that of the Lode Lane trolleybus terminus. Today it stands within the security boundary of the Land Rover factory and thanks must be sincerely expressed to the security police for allowing 2489 (JOJ 489) into the confines of the works. The Crossley is standing outside the original camouflaged brick-built shadow factory that was only completed in the months immediately prior to the outbreak of the Second World War. This original part of the factory is still in use for engineering development work, but little else is the same. The old trolleybus turning loop is now a major intersection within the works road system, while the green fields of 1950 are now covered by large factory buildings. *D. R. Harvey*

On the following Sunday, 24 June 1951, just seven days before the closure, Birmingham's newest trolleybus, 90 (FOK 90), was used by the Omnibus Society on a final farewell tour of the system. As we have already seen, it first travelled to the Arden Oak terminus from Station Street, then turned into Hobs Moat Road junction using its traction batteries for the manoeuvre. It is thought that this tour and the one undertaken on 24 June 1951 were the only times that this was done when carrying passengers. No 90 is seen in the private Rover works road having used the large turning circle in the background. It is standing at the loading point outside the factory buildings and will shortly return to the city. *J. P. Addenbrooke*

*Above* Metro-Cammell-bodied Leyland TTBD2 18 (OC 1118) has just left the unloading stop at the top end of Carrs Lane and has stopped at the junction with High Street. In its last year in service, it is working on the 94 service along Coventry Road to the city boundary. It will turn right in front of Allan's gown shop, and, after using a couple of notches of power in High Street, will make a further turn to the right into Albert Street before coasting down the hill to the loading shelters outside the Beehive Store.

The Birmingham livery was a distinguished deep, dark blue for the lower panels contrasting with the equally subtle shade of creamy primrose. The khaki roof was adopted as standard after the end of the Second World War and replaced the all-over primrose roof. *C. Carter*

*Below* Leyland TTBD2 trolleybus 31 (OC 1131) passes Allen Griffiths's shoe shop in Moor Street working out of the city on a 92 route short working from Albert Street to Yardley. This was the original trolleybus service along Coventry Road, opened on 5 January 1934. The six-wheeler entered service on the same day, so it is appropriate that this rare colour photograph depicts one of these hard-working vehicles. Compare this view with that of 35 (OC 1135) when new in 1934 on page 48. *C. Carter*

The Birmingham blue livery has weathered to a bleached powder blue after 18 years exposed to the elements in Bird's scrapyard at Stratford-upon-Avon. Long after all the other Birmingham trolleybuses had been broken up, the remains of the lower saloons of six-wheeled Leyland TTBD2 29 (OC 1129) and four-wheeler 73 (COX 73), which is lying on its side, were still identifiable in 1969, less than a year before the scrapyard was cleared. Both of these trolleybuses had been taken to Bird's in the spring of 1952, having first gone to Cunliffe's yard in Handsworth. *D. R. Harvey*

The strangest fate that befell four Birmingham trolleybuses was to become motor buses. Two of these conversions took place in the 1930s on nearly new former demonstrators OV 1175 and OV 1194. The second two involved the 11-year-old MCCW bodies of FOK-registered 83 and 90, which were bought from Bird's by Silcox of Pembroke Dock, who mounted the bodies on Bristol K6G chassis (see also page 116). The second one, registered ODE 402, fitted with the body from 83, is seen here in Silcox's garage yard towards the end of its career. Although painted in Silcox's smart red and white livery, its Birmingham origins can still be seen. It lasted longer than its twin, not being withdrawn until 1967. *A. Richardson, Photobus*

An apparently normal though elderly double-decker stands at the Batley Centenary Show about 1969. What most enthusiasts would see as a Leyland 'Titan' TD1 is, in fact, far more unusual, as, when new, it was Leyland Motors' first trolleybus! This was originally OV 1175 and was demonstrated to Birmingham Corporation in 1931. The only clue to its ancestry is the strengthening gusset on the central window pillar which was necessary as this pillar had in it a conduit to carry the main electric wiring from the overhead to the traction motor. The bus is carrying its Jersey registration J 1199, although in 1971 it was re-registered again as MJX 222J. *A. Richardson, Photobus*

# TROLLEYBUS MISCELLANY

## Demonstrators

*Above* The first Leyland trolleybus to be demonstrated to Birmingham was based on a converted Leyland 'Titan' TD1 chassis; it was given the fleet number 19 and registered OV 1175. The project was jointly financed by GEC and Leyland Motors, which fitted GEC's WT25 65hp traction motor to the engineless chassis. The body was built by Short Brothers and was based on the standard 'lowbridge' Leyland design. BCT's interest in the development of replacement trolleybuses for its Railless fleet enabled the Leyland/GEC four-wheeled prototype to be demonstrated on the Nechells route from 20 May until 18 August 1931, when it was returned to Leyland. It is seen here in GEC's Witton works, showing how the electric traction motor occupied the space normally occupied by a Leyland 6.8-litre petrol engine. *R. Marshall*

*Below left* The 'lowbridge' GEC-motored Leyland TBD1 trolleybus was later demonstrated unsuccessfully to Chesterfield Corporation, which instead placed an order for a pair of Ransomes, Simms & Jefferies D2 double-deckers.

The significance of OV 1175 and the slightly later six-wheel demonstrator TJ 939 was that they were the first double-deck trolleybuses manufactured by Leyland Motors. What is surprising is that neither vehicle was demonstrated extensively, and that after appearing in Chesterfield OV 1175 was never seen again - that is as a trolleybus! It underwent something of a metamorphosis, being converted into a petrol-engined Leyland TD1. In February 1934 it was sold to Jersey Motor Traction as its No 25 and registered J 1199, as seen here. The only clue to its trolleybus ancestry is the slightly thicker upper saloon front window pillar, which carried the electric cables from the trolleypole gantry through the Short Brothers body

to the traction motors. The fact that J 1199 survived the German Occupation of the Channel Islands is itself surprising, and it continued to serve the routes out of St Helier until 1958, when it was bought by Colin Shears and placed in store at his Winkleigh Museum in Devon. In the late 1960s work was started on restoring it, and today, as MJX 222J, it is somewhat ironically the sole surviving Birmingham trolleybus. *A. B. Cross*

*Above* The only known external photograph of 19 (OG 9886) was taken at Guy Motors' Wolverhampton works in December 1934, prior to the sale of three former demonstrator Guy BTXs. They are painted in the green and cream livery of the Llanelly & District Electric Supply Co Ltd. The nearest is 18 (UK 8341), which became Llanelly 17, re-registered as TH 5166. Next to it is UK 8948, which was Llanelly 18 as TH 5167, and the furthest vehicle is OG 9886, which was Llanelly 16.

Guy was probably relieved, and even surprised, to be able to sell these three- or four-year-old trolleybuses, as by the mid-1930s their body design was looking rather antiquated. *R. Marshall collection*

*Above right* The demonstrators that came to the city in the 1930-32 period appear to have been registered in Birmingham if their stay was short, while those that remained for any length of time were registered in their town of origin! A Guy BT, with a 'low-bridge' 48-seater Guy body built on Park Royal frames, was demonstrated on the Nechells route from 20 May 1931 for just 12 days, in which time it amassed 939 miles. It was registered OV 1194 and it given the fleet number 20, which was the highest in the old 'trackless' series.

This vehicle was another abortive attempt by Guy Motors to gain orders from Birmingham after its failure to persuade BCT to have any of the six-wheeled BTX chassis. It was returned to Guy and was never used again as a trolleybus, despite being barely

six months old. There are no photographs of it working as a trolleybus, and a considerable amount of detective work was necessary to identify this Guy 'Arab' II 5LW as being 'the last resting place' of the trolleybus's body.

In 1934 OV 1194 had been fitted with a Guy petrol engine and was sold to Trumans of Shirebrook, Nottinghamshire. It ran in this guise until the Ministry of War Transport allocated to the company one of the last-built Guy 'Arab' II chassis. The old trolleybus body was fitted to the new chassis in January 1947 and the 'new' bus was re-registered KRA 668. It ran in this form until 1949 when the chassis was re-bodied, rather unusually for the chassis type, with a 32-seater coach body built by Unity. KRA 668 is seen here in 1948 with the 1931 former trolleybus body, which appears to be largely unaltered except that it is a half-cab. The uneven pillar arrangement behind the front bulkhead suggests that this is where the electric cables were conduited from the trolleypoles to the traction motors. *R. Marshall*

**Above** Leyland Motors produced three prototype trolleybuses in the 1930-32 period. There was a four-wheel single-decker, the TBS1, and a four-wheel double-decker, the TBD1, which came to Birmingham as OV 1175. The third was the six-wheeled TTBD1, registered TJ 939, which had been 'run in' on the South Lancashire Transport system, frequently used by Leyland for this purpose. It came to Birmingham on 11 March 1933 and, as fleet number 17, ran in full BCT livery. It acted as both a Leyland/GEC demonstrator and as a driving instruction vehicle on the Nechells route for nearly five months.

On its first visit to the city it had the experimental series chassis number of 69657. It returned to operate in Birmingham in July 1936 with a new fleet number of 68 and a replacement chassis number of 1654. It ran until 5 January 1937, but was not returned to Leyland Motors until October, and was eventually broken up. During the course of the two visits it ran 28,884 miles.

Its only other demonstration job took place between the two Birmingham visits when it appeared on hire to Nottingham City Transport. In this photograph TJ 939 is still in full BCT livery as it passes through Theatre Square, Nottingham, in May 1933 on the Woollaton service. Nottingham was obviously impressed with the vehicle as it placed an order for 30 TTBD4s in 1934.

The somewhat twilight world in which this vehicle existed is added to by the doubtful origins of its body. This is credited to Massey Brothers of Wigan, but the front profile suggests that it was either a Leyland body of the style built on the four-wheeled TBD2s supplied to Llanelly & District on 1932, or that it was built under licence by Massey to Leyland's design. *G. H. F. Atkins*

**Left** TJ 939 is seen here at Leyland Motors in late 1937. This is the only photograph showing the trolleybus with its later fleet number of 68. It has also been repainted in the simpler unlined livery, which gave it a more modern appearance. *Leyland Motors*

*Top* The Sunbeam Trolleybus Company had been producing trolleybuses for only three years when the 1933 Commercial Motor Show vehicle was delivered to Birmingham. The eighth MS2-type chassis to be manufactured entered service on 10 February 1934, just five weeks after the opening of the Coventry Road routes. Fitted with a metal-framed Metro-Cammell 59-seater body, it was registered in Birmingham as OC 6567.

By the end of March 1934 the trolleybus had operated almost 3,000 miles in the space of seven weeks, a figure that was comparable to the mileages being run by the AEC 663Ts. Sunbeam must have thought that its locally built product would gain substantial orders, but, as with the products of the firm's fellow Wulfrunians at Guy Motors, the BCT staff were not impressed as the Metro-Vickers 80hp motors were non-standard. The trolleybus was returned to Sunbeam and sold to Wolverhampton Corporation for £1,850, where it is seen running on trade-plates almost certainly in Wolverhampton on a trial run for Sunbeam. It was the first BCT bus or trolleybus to have a cream-painted waist-rail, a feature that was adopted in the following year.

It is also reputed that Sunbeam's other exhibit at the 1933 show, a Sunbeam MF2A with a 'lowbridge' Park Royal body, was painted in Birmingham livery with the fleet number 87. This trolleybus did not even get on to the streets of the city, but turned up three years later as Reading Corporation's first trolleybus! *Transport World*

*Middle* Sunbeam MS2 demonstrator 67 (OC 6567) became Wolverhampton Corporation's 222 in September 1934. Nearly 14 years old, it is seen working on the Wednesfield service near New Cross on Tuesday 30 March 1948. It was withdrawn in April 1949. *F. W. Shuttleworth*

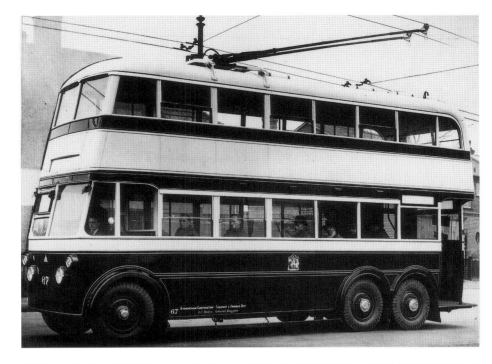

*Bottom* After being withdrawn by Wolverhampton Corporation, OC 6567 turned up as a single-deck caravan at Borth near Aberystwyth, surviving in this guise into the 1960s. In the early post-war years a field of old buses and trolleybuses 'grew' here, used as cheap holiday caravans and chalets when other accommodation was simply too expensive. *R. Marshall*

## A tour around trolleybus 18

*Top* No 18 (OC 1118) is posed before its entry into service. The photograph shows the clean, though conservative styling of these vehicles, which rather belied their stylish and comfortable interiors.

The use of No 18 in the official BCT photographs of the 17-66 Class rather backs up the theory that the first vehicle of the class was the one that was tested on the Nechells route painted in grey primer. No 17 was held back by Metro-Cammell while the rest of the class were completed.

After construction these Leylands were released by Metro-Cammell to the nearby Washwood Heath depot. Each vehicle was then given a test run on the Nechells route. As deliveries began at least one month before the Yardley service opened, most of the trolleybuses numbered from 18 to 65 were stored in the newly opened Perry Barr garage. *BCT*

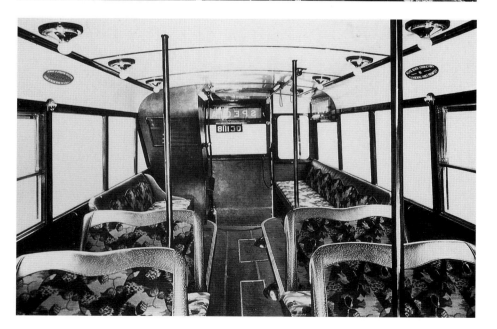

*Middle and bottom* These two views of 18 (OC 1118) show the well-appointed lower saloons of these 1934 Metro-Cammell bodies. The interior design of Birmingham's bus fleet had been developed with the AEC 'Regent' deliveries of 1929 and was continued, with an evolving programme of improvements, until the last of the Crossley-bodied Daimler CVG6s were delivered in October 1954.

The lower saloon was equipped with moquette-covered seats, while the front bulkhead, side panels, staircase and platform area were covered in leather cloth. The extensive use of polished wood on the front bulkhead, window frames and ceiling laths gave a bright, comfortable feel for the passengers sitting on the generously spaced 25 seats. The main difference between these trolleybuses and contemporary bus interiors was the black Doverite-covered stanchion poles. *Courtesy of Travel West Midlands*

*Top and middle* If the lower saloon of a Birmingham bus or trolleybus was the 'lounge', then the upper saloon was the 'smoking room'. The 33 seats and body panels were finished in English antique-style leather cloth, while the wooden fixtures and fittings were the same as those in the lower saloon. These trolleybuses were among the last BCT vehicles to have seat backs with shaped tops. The white-painted ceilings and cove panels would rapidly turn a shade of yellow-brown with the nicotine from the cigarette smoke. *Courtesy of Travel West Midlands*

*Bottom* By way of contrast, the interior of Metro-Cammell-bodied Leyland TB7 90 (FOK 90) is seen at the end of its service life in June 1951. The nicotine-stained ceiling in the upper saloon, as well as the standard arrangement of the fixtures and fittings, shows up well. The interior of these trolleybuses was virtually identical to the contemporary bus bodies; the straight seat backs had been standard since the AOG batch of Daimler COG5s of 1935. *R. Marshall*

## Tilting at Tyburn

Tyburn Road Works was only used for overhauling the trolleybus fleet from December 1929, when it was opened, until the trolleybus fleet repaints went back to Kyotts Lake Road, prior to the conversion of the Coventry Road route.

The mandatory 'typing' of an individual bus of a new class also took place at Tyburn Road, as it had the facility to undertake tilt-tests. The first of the half-cab Leyland TBD2s, 1 (OV 4001), the 1931 Commercial Motor Show exhibit, was taken to the works and tested on 31 December 1931, a full month before it entered service. Perhaps this delay was caused by the vehicles proving to be slightly too heavy. Although it has not yet toppled over, having reached 35 degrees, on other tests with different sand-bag loadings, it did become unstable, necessitating the removal of certain items and reducing the upper saloon seating capacity by one in order to lighten the trolley-buses.

Parked over a pit on the right is 359 (OF 3991), one of the first batch of AEC 'Regent' 661s fitted with Brush H26/24R bodies, but already two years old. With an MoWT-style Brush body fitted in February 1944, it nearly outlasted all BCT's trolley-buses, lasting until June 1950! *Courtesy of Travel West Midlands*

## At 'The Lake'

*Below left* Except from 1929 until about 1933, when Tyburn Road Works was used, trolleybuses were always over-hauled at the tram works at Kyotts Lake Road in Sparkbrook. This reinforces the view that BCT regarded its trolleybuses as 'trams with tyres' rather than 'buses with poles'! Here is a trolleybus on a tram-truck! An unidentified Roe body, possibly from 2 (OK 4832), is seen in Henley Street en route from Sampson Road paintshop to the tram works. It is being towed on a Brill 21E truck by an unidentified passenger car. In the works it will be reunited with its Railless F12-type chassis before being towed back to Washwood Heath depot to resume service. The rear mudguards can be seen in the lower saloon. This photograph was taken before 1928, as the canopy over the driver's cab has been repainted in its original blue livery. On their final repaint, at Tyburn Road, the canopy was painted cream in the same style as the buses. *D. F. Potter collection*

*Opposite top* The upper saloon of the trolleybus fleet was always referred to on the legal lettering as the 'outside saloon', again reflecting the fact that they were overhauled at the tram works and regarded as 'trackless trams'. However, Alfred Baker, the city's first transport General Manager, always referred to them as 'Trolley Vehicles'.

In July 1950 Leyland TB7 84 (FOK 84) has been given what BCT coyly designated

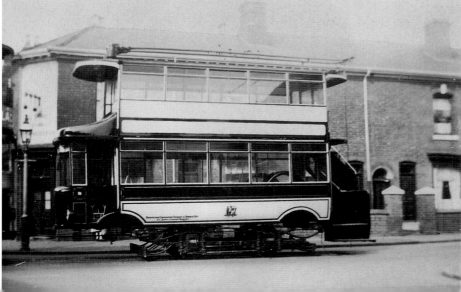

'a light touch-up and varnish'. In the paintshop are also one of the six-wheeled trolleys and two of Cotteridge depot's Short Brothers-bodied, Maley & Taunton air-brake cars; car 834 is behind the trolley-bus and 817 is to the right.

The trolleybuses reached Kyotts Lake Road in three ways, none of which was really convenient! The Nechells trolleybuses used the Washwood Heath tram route all the way to the city, using the trailing skate throughout the journey! Except for the six years of overlap between 1934 and 1940, the Nechells trolleybuses went all the way to the works under their own skate power. At first the Coventry Road trolleys reached Kyotts Lake Road under their own power; they were de-poled at Bordesley railway bridge and employed a short section of trolleybus overhead that went left into Camp Hill. Here they were attached to the tram wire and used the Stratford Road tram tracks and a skate to get to 'The Lake'. After 1937 the trolleys could go to Rea Street and turn left into Bradford Street and reach Camp Hill with a skate in the tram track. These manoeuvres did occur, but it seems that in later years the vehicles were towed to the works. *R. F. Mack*

# Bird's and after

*Middle* Bird's undertook to tow the 61 trolleybuses to Stratford-upon-Avon between Saturday 30 June and Sunday 1 July 1951. The towing vehicles employed were a variety of ex-Second World War military vehicles. Most common was the AEC 'Matador', but other vehicles were used. Pausing for a break in the countryside on the A34, the leading trolleybus, 37 (OC 1137), is being towed by a Commer Q4 4x2 3-tonner, which was basically a pre-war 'Superpoise' model fitted with a WD body. The second trolleybus is being towed by an ex-US Army Studebaker 6x6 2.5-ton truck.

The trolleybuses were apparently towed along the A34 through Solihull and Henley. How they managed to get underneath the Stratford-upon-Avon aqueduct at Wootton Wawen and the railway bridge at Bearley is a matter of conjecture. *J. Whybrow collection*

*Bottom* Exactly five months after the abandonment of the trolleybuses in Birmingham, John Hughes and the late Cliff Brown visited Bird's scrapyard in Stratford. The trolleybus fleet were parked with their tyres still inflated as if all that was required to make them run again was a set of overhead wires!

Six-wheeler 33 (OC 1133) stands next to an unidentified member of the 79-90 Class at the front of three rows of trolleybuses. Bird's tried to sell the four-wheeled Leyland TB7s to an overseas operator, rumoured to be in South Africa, but the deal fell through and they were broken up with the rest of the fleet over the next two years. *C. Brown*

*Above left* By the summer of 1952 the scene at Bird's had changed dramatically. With their trolleybooms blowing in the wind, the trolleybuses had been stripped of their tyres and glass as a concerted start was made at removing their aluminium roof panels and reduce them to their skeletal frames. On the left is 58 (OC 1158), while in front of the anonymous 79-90 Class Leyland TB7, identifiable by its nearside trafficator fitment, is 69 (COX 69), one of the 1937 Leyland TB5s. *K. Moody*

*Above right* The 11-year-old Metro-Cammell-bodied Leyland TB7s of 1940 deserved perhaps a better fate than being broken up at Bird's former brickworks and quarry alongside the main A34 in Stratford-upon-Avon. Despite attempts to sell them, only two partially escaped the breaker's torch. Nos 83 (FOK 83) and 90 (FOK 90) were sold to W. L. Silcox of Pembroke Dock. Silcox had managed to order 11 single-deck and six double-deck chassis from Bristol before that chassis manufacturer was nationalised in 1948, making them unobtainable on the open market. Silcox built a number of rather eccentrically designed bodies themselves, but still required more. Having purchased the two trolleybuses, they placed the refurbished bodies on two of their Bristol K6G chassis. ODE 401 received the body from trolleybus 90, and with the

exception of the full front and the Bristol radiator, it retained its Birmingham character, even keeping the three sets of mouldings until it was withdrawn in September 1961. *A. Porter collection*

## 'The King is dead - long live the King'

*Below* On Saturday 30 June 1951 the last trolleybuses were prepared for service as per normal. This was the last day of trolleybus operation on the 94 service along Coventry Road, as the last Lode Lane services had run during the previous evening. Leyland TB7 82 (FOK 82), to the left of the pillar, waits to go into service for the last time, while in the background stand the new replacement Daimler CVD6s with Metro-Cammell bodies. On the right the first of the Leyland six-wheelers, 17 (OC 1117), along with several other trolleybuses, had already been taken out of service and has had its fleet number painted out and its destination blinds removed.

No 2639 (JOJ 639) stands at the front of the nearest line of Daimler-engined Daimlers. These were appropriate replacements as they were the quietest and most refined diesel-engined buses available in the fleet. *N. S. Stone*

By the evening of 30 June 1951 the replacement buses had begun to take the space of the departing trolleybuses in Coventry Road garage. The new buses belonged to the 2626-2775 batch of Daimler CVD6s, and Nos 2646, 2640, 2639 and 2647, all with matching JOJ registrations, can be identified here. In the background is numerically Birmingham's last trolleybus, 90 (FOK 90), which only one week before had been hired for the Omnibus Society's Farewell Tour and later the same evening would perform the funeral rites on the system. *D. R. Harvey collection*

## The last one!

After the last service trolleybuses, 73 (COX 73) and its duplicate, 45 (OC 1145), left Albert Street at 11.02 pm, they were followed by the last trolleybus. This had left Coventry Road depot at 10.45 pm with the General Manager, W. H. Smith, members of the Transport Department and honoured guests. The conductor decided to go around the dignitaries on the trolleybus and, in lieu of other instructions, made everyone pay full fare!

The trolleybuses went out with a whimper as far as the general public were concerned, although many of the passengers on 73 and 45 were trolleybus devotees. However, at the depot the trolleybus staff had a farewell party, which started at about 8.30 pm and lasted until the small hours of the morning. Almost certainly the last trolleybus was 90 (FOK 90), although the records of the event are very sketchy. It was driven by Mr F. L. Gilks, who is seen in the cab of the still illuminated Metro-Cammell-bodied Leyland as it stands inside the depot at about 12.05 am on 1 July 1951. In front of him are the depot party-goers.

Soon it would all be over! There was another photograph taken a few minutes later of the official party, and by 12.30 the power was switched off for the last time. *D. F. Potter collection*

## Replacement buses

*Above* Standing in the Yardley trolleybus turning circle not long after the trolleybus closure is 1969 (HOV 969). This handsome Metro-Cammell-bodied exposed-radiator Daimler CVD6 dates from 1949, and is working on the 57B route between Station Street and Yardley, which was a direct replacement for the 93 trolleybus service. *W. A. Camwell*

*Below left* The new Daimler CVD6s were placed in service on Sunday 1 July 1951. The normal BCT practice was to remove the overhead within days of the closure of a route, but Derek Griffiths managed to photograph one of these new buses, 2647 (JOJ 647), beneath the de-energised trolleybus wires in Hay Mills near the Kings Road junction on its way into the city. It is working on the newly introduced 60 service to Cranes Park Estate, whose residents had been clamouring for a trolleybus service since before the Lode Lane branch had been introduced during the Second World War. *D. Griffiths*

*Below* The replacement buses were extremely smart. Positively gleaming in Hay Mills near Kings Road is Daimler CVD6 2633 (JOJ 633), with a Metro-Cammell 54-seater body, working on the 58 route. These 150 buses of the 2626 Class were the first 'standard' BCT design to have one-piece metal-framed bodywork; all previous Birmingham metal-framed body orders had their bodies built in two halves. The trolleybus fleet was partially replaced by the first 30 of these Daimlers, which entered service on 1 July 1951 from Coventry Road garage. *D. R. Harvey collection*

## Trolleybus destination blinds

*Right* Washwood Heath depot's destination blind had just four displays, of which the top two were most frequently used. From 1932 until about 1937, this blind was only used in the five AEC 663Ts, as with their weight problems the Leyland TBD1s could only employ paper stickers.

*Below* The 1936 extension to the City Boundary at Sheldon added the 94 and 95 services to the original four Coventry Road services. This blind also had the Nechells destinations on it; with the limited amount of vehicle exchanges that did occur in the 1938 to 1940 period, it was useful to have a common destination blind. This blind became redundant in October 1940, with the suspension of the Nechells service.

*Below right* This is a standard Coventry Road trolleybus blind, with the Wagon Lane turn-back route 99 having been added in 1949. It also has the 56 and 57 short workings to Hay Mills and the original 92 and 93 services to Yardley. Additionally, the two sets of workings to both the City Boundary, 94 and 95, and to Lode Lane, 96 and 97, from the two city termini in Albert Street and Station Street are also on the blind. *Blinds courtesy of D. F. Potter, photographs D. R. Harvey*

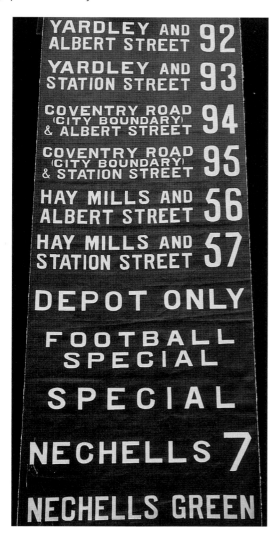

## Driver Gilks

These newspaper cuttings from the *Birmingham Mail* of 26 June 1951 entitled 'B'ham's Last Trolley Buses Will "Emigrate" and 'Farewell To The Trolleys' both give detailed information about the events of Saturday 30 June 1951.
Birmingham Mail

# B'ham's Last Trolley Buses Will 'Emigrate'

Special police will be on duty outside Coventry Road transport depot to guard against boisterous souvenir hunters when the last of Birmingham's trolley buses brings the Coventry Road service to an end about midnight on Saturday.

All the buses have been sold to a contractor and most of the servicable vehicles will be converted to fuel-oil buses and shipped to South Africa. There they will be used to transport native workers to the mines.

The honour of driving the last trolley bus will go appropriately to Driver Frederick Leonard Gilks. Driver Gilks will be 62 on

July 18, and was due to retire in May but, owing to staff shortages postponed his retirement until the change-over from trolleys to fuel-oil buses had been completed.

He lives at 242 Monica Road, Small Heath, and began with the Transport Department in May, 1911, as a conductor.

He told "The Birmingham Mail" to-day that his first duties were on the cross-city route from Small Heath to Nechells. After two years conducting he became a tram driver and was on the trams until the trolley buses replaced them on January 7, 1934.

"Throughout my 40 years with the Corporation," he said, "I have been at the Coventry Road depot, except for a period during the first World War, when I served in the Coldstream Guards. For 30 years I have not lost an accident free bonus."

### Farewell Party

Driver Gilks' bus will be boarded at the depot by members of the Birmingham Transport Committee and senior officials of the department who have been invited to make the last and historic journey between Albert Street and the city boundary at Sheldon.

All the staff at Coventry Road depot are to join in a farewell party at the depot on Saturday night, and the festivities will began at 8.30. as the trolley buses begin to come into depot after completing their final runs.

When fuel-oil buses begin to operate along the Coventry Road on Sunday morning, a new service will be inaugurated serving the rapidly growing municipal estate at Cranes Park.

The former 96, Lode Lane, trolley service will not be replaced by buses. as this route is outside the city. It will be served by the Midland "Red," who already operate a cross-country service from Marston Green to Solihull.

The change-over involves the replacement of 64 trolley buses.

Driver F. L. Gilks, who is to drive the last Coventry Road trolley bus on Saturday night, getting into the driving cab of his vehicle at the start of his first run from depot to-day.

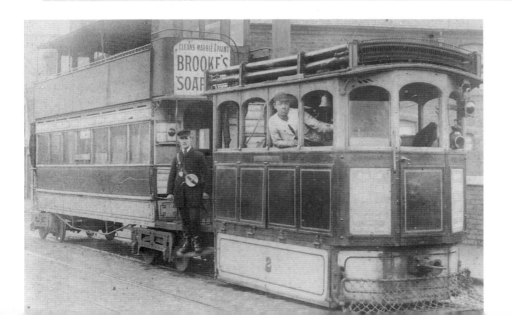

The driver of the last trolleybus, 45 (O 1145), was Driver Frederick Leonard Gilks During research I was able to examine th excellent John Whybrow Collection of ol photographs of Birmingham and found most unusual coincidence. This view c CBT Kitson steam locomotive No 2, repu edly in Small Heath, has as its conducto one Fred Gilks. Although the photograph i dated 1910, it has to be before 23 Februar 1905 as this is when steam tram operatio ceased on Coventry Road. Could the con ductor be the same person as the driver o Birmingham's last trolleybus? There cer tainly appears to be a family resemblance It would be most gratifying if this was th last trolleybus driver seen 45 years earlie in his youth. *John Whybrow collection*

# FAREWELL TO THE TROLLEYS

## "New Look" Buses for Birmingham

### 30 WILL BE ON ROAD TO-MORROW

Thirty "new look" fuel-oil buses, which have yet to carry their first passenger, are waiting in the Coventry Road, Birmingham, bus depot—the nucleus of the fleet of buses which will replace the familiar trolley buses after to-day.

Birmingham, which was the first municipal transport undertaking to use trolley buses, is now among the first to abandon them.

For the past 18 months, drivers at the Coventry Road depot have been receiving tuition in the driving of fuel-oil buses ready for the change-over.

### Last Ride

Altogether, 64 trolley buses will be scrapped and the entire fleet of buses which will operate from the Coventry Road depot will be post-war models.

The last trolley bus will leave the depot at 10.30 to-night, and will drive into town carrying four members of the Transport Committee and senior officials of the department, including the general manager, Mr. W. H. Smith.

Mr. Smith told "The Birmingham Mail" to-day: "I wouldn't miss a trip on the last trolley for anything. I have not missed one of these change-overs since the policy of replacing trams and trolley buses by fuel-oil buses was begun. To-day is an historic day for the department and marks a great step forward. I hope to be on Birmingham's last tram ride, too."

### Farewell Party

As the last trolley buses come into depot this evening the drivers, conductors and conductresses and depot staff will start a farewell party which will last until the small hours.

The climax of the evening's fun will be the arrival at the depot of the last trolley bus at about midnight, carrying the official party. It will be driven by Mr. F. L. Gilks, who will be 62 next month, and is to retire after 40 years with the Birmingham transport undertaking.

Special police will be on duty to restrain would-be souvenir hunters.

When fuel-oil buses begin operating to-morrow morning a new service will begin operation along the Coventry Road, serving the rapidly-expanding new municipal estate at Cranes Park.

---

# Extract from the Drivers' Rule Book

This extract from the Birmingham Corporation Tramways & Omnibus Department's Rule Book refers specifically to trolleybus driving. The apparently easy task of driving a trolleybus was in reality rather difficult and required considerable skill, as can be seen here from all the restrictions and sequences of which drivers had to be aware.

## 46

## Supplementary Rules
### FOR TROLLEY 'BUS DRIVERS.

*(Also see pages 17 to 34 and 42 to 45—where applicable).*

**Examination of Trolley 'Bus before leaving Depot.**

1. See that all switches are in the "off" position.

2. When necessary, see that Skate Cable is properly connected to the bracket on 'bus body and place skate in groove of rail.

3. Put trolleys properly on wire.

4. Test lights, including headlights, and red rear lamp, and examine emergency lamps.

5. Make sure that the foot brake goes on before pedal reaches the footboard and that the handbrake is holding when lever is half-way up the quadrant.

6. Make sure that rubber gloves, rope with clamp, and section box and telephone keys are in proper place.

7. See that wheel scotch, bamboo pole and skate stick are in their proper places.

8. Examine fire extinguishers and see that they are full.

9. Remove any stones, glass, etc., that may be embedded in the tyres.

10. Try horn and Conductors' signal bell.

## SUPPLEMENTARY RULES.  47

11. Examine lifeguards, destination indicators, mirrors and screen wipers.

12. Inspect 'bus generally for freshly made marks, scratches, broken windows, etc., and report any defects to the Shed Superintendent or Foreman.

13. Examine jack box and see that seal is unbroken.

14. See that all switches are correctly set and brake gauge is in order.

**Attention to skates and trolleys.** Drivers must see that proper attention is given to trolleys and skates at all times. Before changing from skate to trolley, or trolley to skate, all switches are to be "out."

**Leaving 'Bus.** Drivers should not leave their 'bus unless absolutely necessary. When a driver has occasion to leave his cabin the switches are to be put to the "off" position, and the hand brake correctly and tightly applied. If a 'bus is left on a gradient the steering wheel must be turned so that the front wheels point to the kerb. The scotch is to be placed under the rear wheel.

**Approaching cross-roads.** When approaching a dangerous cross road the power pedal must be at the "off" position.

**Descending gradients.** When descending gradients the hand brake must be kept sufficiently applied to keep the 'bus well in hand, and the speed controlled by the foot brake, thus leaving both hands free for the steering wheel.

**Passing under tramway trolley wire.** Where the tramway overhead wiring crosses that of the 'buses, drivers are not to attempt to pass under the short dead section until the road is quite clear, so as to avoid possibility of stopping with the pole on the dead wire.

# THE BIRMINGHAM TROLLEYBUS FLEET

## Fleet details

Columnar information is given in the following order: fleet number, registration number, chassis number (where known) and career details.

D = delivered; RN = re-numbered; W = withdrawn; S = sold; BU = broken up; SRdN = Sampson Road North paintshop

### 1-12, OK 4823-4834; Railless F12

**Motors:** 2 x 42hp DK 85A series-wound. One per driven wheel. No differential. 1 x EEC Form D hand-controller.
**Body:** C. Roe H25/26ROS.

| 1 | OK 4823 | ? | Tested out on Leeds Corporation trackless on Guiseley-Otley route 13/7/22. D 7/10/22. W 1/2/32. BU -/32. |
| 2 | OK 4824 | ? | D 12/10/22. W 1/2/32. BU -/32. |
| 3 | OK 4825 | ? | D 16/10/22. W 2/32. BU -/32. |
| 4 | OK 4826 | ? | D 20/11/22. RN as 13 1/2/32. W 18/8/32. S 22/3/33. |
| 5 | OK 4827 | ? | D 26/10/22. W 1/2/32. BU -/32. |
| 6 | OK 4828 | ? | D 30/10/22. W 1/2/32. BU -/32. |
| 7 | OK 4829 | ? | D 4/11/22. W 4/11/22. BU -/32. |
| 8 | OK 4830 | ? | D 9/11/22. RN as 15 1/2/32. W 31/8/32. S 22/3/33. |
| 9 | OK 4831 | ? | D 13/11/22. W 3/2/32. BU -/32. |
| 10 | OK 4832 | ? | D 18/11/22. W 3/2/32. BU -/32. |
| 11 | OK 4833 | ? | D 24/11/22. W 4/2/32. BU -/32. |
| 12 | OK 4834 | ? | D 1/12/22. W 31.8.32. S 22/3/33. |

### 13, OL 994; AEC 602

**Motors:** 2 x 42hp BTH GE 247A series-wound. 1 x BTH hand-controller.
**Body:** Brush B36R.

| 13 | OL 994 | 602.005 | D -/23. |

AEC Ltd, Southall, demonstrator 17/8/23-10/23, in red livery. Probably became Mexborough & Swinton 31, 12/24. W -/29.

### 13, OL 4636; EMB

**Motors:** 2 x 42hp DK 85A series-wound. EEC Form D hand-controllers.
**Body:** C. Roe H28/20R.

| 13 | OL 4636 | ? | D 10/4/24. |

EMB, West Bromwich, demonstrator. Exhibited in Nottingham. On hire to BCT 4/24- 21/4/26. Returned to EMB 29/6/28 and BU.

### –, TO 5011; Railless LF

**Motors:** 2 x 35hp DK99A series-wound. One per driven wheel. No differential. EEC Form D foot-controller.
**Body:** Short H26/26ROS.

| - | TO 5011 | ? | D -/25. |

1925 CMS exhibit. Intended for BCT but not delivered as it wa[s] fitted with foot-controllers. To Nottingham Corporation -/26 a[s] 10. W -/34. To ?, Ashover.

### 14-16, ON 2825-2827; Railless LF

**Motors:** 2 x 35hp DK99A series-wound. One per drive[n] wheel. No differential. EEC Form D hand-controllers.
**Body:** Short H25/26ROS.

| 14 | ON 2825 | ? | D 6/3/26. W 31/8/32. S 22/3/33. |
| 15 | ON 2826 | ? | D 12/3/26. W 2/32. BU -/32. |
| 16 | ON 2827 | ? | D 16/3/26. W 3/32. BU -/32. |

### 17, ON 3261; AEC 607

**Motor:** 1 x 55hp Bull series-wound. Driven through dif[ferential]. EMB foot-controller.
**Body:** Vickers H26/26ROS.

| 17 | ON 3261 | 607001 | |

AEC, Southall, demonstrator 3/26. Purchased by BCT -/26. W 31/8/32. S 22/3/33.

### 18, UK 8341; Guy BTX

**Motor:** 1 x 60hp Rees-Roturbo compound-wound. Rees[-]Stevens controller (made by BTH).
**Body:** Guy H27/26R.

| 18 | UK 8341 | BTX 23456 | D 1/30. |

Guy Motors, Wolverhampton, demonstrator, 22/2/30-31/5/31[.] Returned to Guy Motors 9/31. To Llanelly & District Electri[c] Supply Co Ltd, Llanelly, as 17, 1/35. Re-reg TH 5166. T[o] H33/27R 1/35. W -/45. To Balfour Beatty, 12/46-c.5/49 as work[-]man's hut at Carmarthen Bay Power Station.

### 19, OG 9886; Guy BTX

**Motor:** 1 x 75hp Rees-Roturbo compound-wound. Rees[-]Stevens controller (made by BTH).
**Body:** Guy H27/26R (straight staircase).

| 19 | OG 9886 | BTX 23648 | D 3/31. |

Guy Motors, Wolverhampton, demonstrator, 10/4/31-17/4/31[.] Returned to Guy Motors 4/31. To Llanelly & District Electri[c] Supply Co Ltd, Llanelly, as 16, 1/35. To H31/28R 1/35. T[o] Davies & Davies (dealer), Burry Port, 12/46. To caravan, Burr[y] Port Sands, Carmarthenshire 1947-80.

### 19, OV 1175; Leyland TBD1 (prototype Leyland four[-]wheeler)

**Motor:** 1 x 65hp GEC WT 265 series-wound. GEC FA3[?] controller.
**Body:** Short Bros L24/24R (to Leyland design); half cab.

| 19 | OV 1175 | 60342 | D 1/31. |

Leyland Motors, Leyland, demonstrator. First tested on Sout[h] Lancs Transport system. To BCT 20/5/31-18/8/31. Returned t[o]

Leyland Motors 8/31. Demonstrated to Chesterfield Corp 8/31. To Leyland Motors and converted to TD1 petrol-engined chassis. To Jersey Motors as 25, J 1199, 2/34. W 1958. To C. Shears, Winkleigh, for preservation. Re-reg MJX 222J.

## 20, OV 1194; Guy BT
**Motor:** 1 x 60hp Rees-Roturbo compound-wound. Rees-Stevens controller (made by BTH).
**Body:** Guy/Park Royal L24/24R.

| | | | |
|---|---|---|---|
| 20 | OV 1194 | BT 23747 | D 4/31. |

Guy Motors, Wolverhampton, demonstrator 20/5/31-31/5/31. To Guy Motors; converted to FC petrol-engined chassis c-/34. To Truman, Shirebrook, -/34. W 10/47. Chassis BU. Body to KRA 668, Guy 'Arab' II, 5LW -/47. Rebodied Unity C32F, 4/49. To Musgrave Motor Coaches, South Kirkby, 9/57. To T. D. Alexander (Greyhound) as 51, 3/58-5/59. To Johnson, Worksop, -/60 and BU.

## 1-3/5-7/9-11/13/15, OV 4001-3/5-7/9-11/13/15; Leyland TBD1
**Motor:** 1 x 65hp GEC WT251 series-wound. GEC FA3B controllers.
**Body:** Short Bros H27/21R, half-cab.

| | | | |
|---|---|---|---|
| 1 | OV 4001 | 72222 | D 2/2/32. Exhibited at 1931 CMS. W 30/9/40. Stored at SRdN 10/40-6/45. To Midland Motors, Small Heath, 3/5/46. To Holland (dealer), Oldbury, 9/6/50 and BU by c-/51. |
| 2 | OV 4002 | 72223 | D 2/2/32. W 30/9/40. Stored at SRdN 10/40-6/45. To Midland Motors, Small Heath, 3/5/46 and BU. |
| 3 | OV 4003 | 72224 | As No 2. |
| 5 | OV 4005 | 72231 | D 2/2/32. W 29/2/40, then as No 2. |
| 6 | OV 4006 | 72226 | D 3/2/32, then as No 2. |
| 7 | OV 4007 | 72224 | As No 6. |
| 9 | OV 4009 | 72227 | D 5/2/32, then as No 2. |
| 10 | OV 4010 | 72232 | D 4/2/32, then as No 2. |
| 11 | OV 4011 | 72229 | D 5/2/32. Numerically at least this was the extra vehicle added to the original order for ten trolleybuses. W 29/2/40. Later stored at SRdN to 6/45. To Midland Motors Small Heath, 3/5/46. Resold to ? (farmer), ?, Vale of Evesham, Worcs, c-/51. |
| 13 | OV 4013 | 72228 | D 5/2/32. Renumbered 4, 2/32, then as No 2. |
| 15 | OV 4015 | 72230 | D 6/2/32. Renumbered 8, 2/32. W 29/2/40, then as No 2. To Holland (dealer), Oldbury, 9/6/50 and BU c-/51. |

## 12-16, OJ 1012-1016; AEC 663T
**Motor:** 1 x 80hp English Electric DK130F series-wound. English Electric controller.
**Body:** Brush H33/25R.

| | | | |
|---|---|---|---|
| 12 | OJ 1012 | 663T066 | D 2/9/32. W 30/9/40. Stored at SRdN to 6/45. To Midland Motors, Small Heath, 3/5/46 and BU. |
| 13 | OJ 1013 | 663T067 | D 19/8/32, then as No 12. |
| 14 | OJ 1014 | 663T068 | D 1/9/32, then as No 12. |
| 15 | OJ 1015 | 663T069 | D 8/9/32, then as No 12. |
| 16 | OJ 1016 | 663T070 | D 6/9/32. Chassis built 5/30 originally as 663T002 with EEC H33/27R body. Rebodied EEC H31/24D, -/31. Exhibited at 1931 CMS. Demonstrated to BCT 28/6/32. Returned to AEC, |

rebuilt as 663T070 and rebodied with Brush H33/25R. W 30/9/40, then as No 12. To Holland (dealer), Oldbury, by 9/6/50 and BU.

## 87, (RD 8085); Sunbeam MF2A
**Motor:** 1 x 80hp BTH 202 compound-wound. BTH controllers.
**Body:** Park Royal L24/26R.

| | | | |
|---|---|---|---|
| 87 | (RD 8085) | R13001MF2. B.3424 | |

Exhibited at 1933 CMS in BCT livery. Never operated by BCT. Demonstrated to Reading Corp 11/35. To Reading Corp as 1, RD 8085, 31/3/36. W 23/3/49. To Lewis (dealer), Maidenhead, 6/50 and BU.

## 17, TJ 939; Leyland TTBD1 (prototype Leyland six-wheeler)
**Motor:** 1 x 65hp GEC WT257 series-wound. GEC FA3A controller.
**Body:** Leyland H34/26R.

| | | | |
|---|---|---|---|
| 17 | TJ 939 | 69657 | D 1/33. |

Leyland Motors, Leyland, demonstrator. Demonstrated to South Lancs Transport -/33. To BCT 11/3/33-31/7/33. Demonstrated to City of Nottingham Transport 5/9/35-9/9/35. Returned to BCT as 68 (TJ 939) (qv).

## 17-66, OC 1117-1166; Leyland TTBD2
**Motor:** 1 x 65hp GEC WT254c series-wound. GEC FA3B controller.
**Body:** MCCW H33/25R (MCCW body contract 36).

| | | | |
|---|---|---|---|
| 17 | OC 1117 | 3164 | D 25/3/34. Almost certainly the vehicle tested on Nechells route 10/33 on T/P 098VP painted in grey primer. W 30/6/51. To Cunliffe (dealer), Handsworth, 7/51. To Bird, Stratford, -/52 and BU. |
| 18 | OC 1118 | 3163 | D 7/1/34. W 30/6/51. To Bird, Stratford, 7/51 and BU. |
| 19 | OC 1119 | 3165 | As No 18. |
| 20 | OC 1120 | 3166 | As No 18. |
| 21 | OC 1121 | 3168 | As No 18. |
| 22 | OC 1122 | 3167 | As No 18. |
| 23 | OC 1123 | 3180 | As No 18. |
| 24 | OC 1124 | 3169 | As No 18. |
| 25 | OC 1125 | 3172 | As No 18. |
| 26 | OC 1126 | 3171 | As No 18. |
| 27 | OC 1127 | 3179 | As No 18. |
| 28 | OC 1128 | 3176 | As No 18. |
| 29 | OC 1129 | 3175 | As No 18, then to Cunliffe (dealer), Handsworth, 7/51. To Bird, Stratford, -/52 and BU. |
| 30 | OC 1130 | 3173 | D 7/1/34, then as No 29. |
| 31 | OC 1131 | 3174 | D 7/1/34. W 31/3/51, then as No 18. |
| 32 | OC 1132 | 3177 | As No 18. |
| 33 | OC 1133 | 3178 | As No 18. |
| 34 | OC 1134 | 3181 | D 7/1/34. Probably painted grey in wartime. W 30/6/51, then as No 18. |
| 35 | OC 1135 | 3187 | As No 18. |
| 36 | OC 1136 | 3185 | As No 18. |
| 37 | OC 1137 | 3191 | D 7/1/34. Air raid damage 7/12/40, then as No 18. |
| 38 | OC 1138 | 3184 | As No 18. |
| 39 | OC 1139 | 3189 | D 7/1/34. Probably painted grey in wartime. W 30/6/51, then as No 18. |

| | | | |
|---|---|---|---|
| 40 | OC 1140 | 3192 | As No 18. |
| 41 | OC 1141 | 3194 | As No 18. |
| 42 | OC 1142 | 3193 | As No 29. |
| 43 | OC 1143 | 3170 | As No 18. |
| 44 | OC 1144 | 3196 | As No 18. |
| 45 | OC 1145 | 3190 | D 7/1/34. Closed Lode Lane branch 29/6/51. Last passenger trolleybus on Coventry Road 30/6/51. W 1/7/51, then as No 18. |
| 46 | OC 1146 | 3182 | As No 18. |
| 47 | OC 1147 | 3183 | As No 18. |
| 48 | OC 1148 | 3201 | As No 18. |
| 49 | OC 1149 | 3188 | As No 29. |
| 50 | OC 1150 | 3195 | As No 18. |
| 51 | OC 1151 | 3198 | As No 18. |
| 52 | OC 1152 | 3206 | As No 18. |
| 53 | OC 1153 | 3202 | As No 18. |
| 54 | OC 1154 | 3197 | As No 18. |
| 55 | OC 1155 | 3199 | As No 29. |
| 56 | OC 1156 | 3204 | As No 18. |
| 57 | OC 1157 | 3203 | As No 18. |
| 58 | OC 1158 | 3200 | As No 18. |
| 59 | OC 1159 | 3209 | As No 18. |
| 60 | OC 1160 | 3210 | As No 29. |
| 61 | OC 1161 | 3186 | As No 18. |
| 62 | OC 1162 | 3205 | As No 29. |
| 63 | OC 1163 | 3208 | D 9/1/34. Fitted with front-dome ventilators, then as No 18. |
| 64 | OC 1164 | 3207 | D 9/1/34, then as No 18. |
| 65 | OC 1165 | 3211 | D 9/1/34, then as No 18. |
| 66 | OC 1166 | 3212 | D 1/3/34. Interior lighting circuits wired into battery supply in order to test for dead sections in the overhead wiring. Probably fitted with traction batteries. Then as No 18. |

## 67, OC 6567; Sunbeam MS2

**Motor:** 1 x 80hp BTH 201BY compound-wound. BTH controller.
**Body:** MCCW H31/28R (MCCW body contract 24).

| | | | |
|---|---|---|---|
| 67 | OC 6567 | 12008 | D 2/33. |

Sunbeam Motors Co Ltd, Wolverhampton, demonstrator 10/2/34-31/3/34. To Wolverhampton Corp Transport as 222, 9/34. W 4/49. To Ankritt (private owner), Walsall, 4/49. Cut down to single-deck. Converted to caravan at Borth, Cardiganshire.

## 68, TJ 939; Leyland TTBD1

**Motor:** 1 x 65hp GEC WT 254c series-wound. GEC FA3A controller.
**Body:** Leyland H34/26R.

| | | | |
|---|---|---|---|
| 68 | TJ 939 | 1654 | D 1/33. |

Leyland Motors, Leyland, demonstrator. Re-motored ex-BCT 17 (qv). Returned to BCT 26/5/36. Demonstrated 9/7/36-30/9/37. To Leyland Motors 1/10/37 and BU.

## 67-78, COX 67-78; Leyland TB5

**Motor:** 1 x 80hp GEC WT2516J series-wound. GEC FA3A controller. Fitted with traction batteries.
**Body:** MCCW H29/24R (MCCW body contract 146).

| | | | |
|---|---|---|---|
| 67 | COX 67 | 13103 | D 9/9/37. W mid-6/51. To Bird, Stratford, 7/51 and BU. |
| 68 | COX 68 | 13105 | D 9/9/37. W 30/6/51. To Bird, Stratford, 7/51 and BU. |
| 69 | COX 69 | 13104 | As No 68. |

| | | | |
|---|---|---|---|
| 70 | COX 70 | 13109 | D 11/9/37, then as No 68. |
| 71 | COX 71 | 13108 | D 13/9/37, then as No 68. |
| 72 | COX 72 | 13107 | D 16/9/37, then as No 68. |
| 73 | COX 73 | 13106 | D 18/9/37. Last official 94 service trolleybus 30/6/51. W 30/6/51. To Cunliffe (dealer), Handsworth, 7/51. To Bird, Stratford, -/52 and BU. |
| 74 | COX 74 | 13112 | D 21/9/37, then as No 68. |
| 75 | COX 75 | 13110 | D 22/9/37, then as No 68. |
| 76 | COX 76 | 13111 | D 24/9/37, then as No 68. |
| 77 | COX 77 | 13113 | D 2/10/37. Air raid damage 14/9/40, then as No 67. |
| 78 | COX 78 | 13114 | D 5/10/37, then as No 68. |

## 79-90, FOK 79-90; Leyland TB7

**Motor:** 1 x 80hp GEC WT2516P series-wound. GEC FA3A controller. Fitted with traction batteries.
**Body:** MCCW H30/24R (MCCW body contract 224).

| | | | |
|---|---|---|---|
| 79 | FOK 79 | 303354 | D 22/1/40. W 30/6/51. To Cunliffe (dealer), Handsworth, 7/51. To Bird, Stratford, -/52 and BU. |
| 80 | FOK 80 | 303359 | D 22/1/40. W 30/6/51. To Bird, Stratford, 7/51 and BU. |
| 81 | FOK 81 | 303361 | D 15/2/40, then as No 80. |
| 82 | FOK 82 | 303362 | D 16/2/40, then as No 79 |
| 83 | FOK 83 | 303360 | D 15/2/40. W 30/6/51. To Bird, Stratford, 7/51. To Silcox, Pembroke Dock, -/51. Body to Bristol K6G, C-80053, as 25, ODE 402, -/52 as FH32/28R. In service 6/52--/67. BU c7/69. Trolleybus chassis and electrical equipment returned to Bird -/51 and BU. |
| 84 | FOK 84 | 303356 | D 20/2/40, then as No 79. |
| 85 | FOK 85 | 303363 | D 16/2/40, then as No 80. |
| 86 | FOK 86 | 303364 | D 16/2/40, then as No 80. |
| 87 | FOK 87 | 303353 | D 19/2/40, then as No 80. |
| 88 | FOK 88 | 303358 | D 27/2/40. W early 6/51, then as No 80. |
| 89 | FOK 89 | 303357 | D 29/2/40, then as No 80. |
| 90 | FOK 90 | 303355 | D 20/2/40. Used for both Omnibus Society and LRTL tours, 6/51. Closed system by 1/7/51. W 1/7/51. To Bird, Stratford, 7/51. To Silcox, Pembroke Dock, -/51. Body to Bristol K6G, C-80052, ODE 401, -/52 as FH32/28R. In service 5/52. MCCW body removed 9/61 and eventually BU. ODE 401 rebodied Willowbrook L27/28R, B.8409, ex-Trent MT AEC 'Regent' 0661, RC 8409. Trolleybus chassis and electrical equipment to Bird -/51 and BU. |

# Trolleybus scale drawings and wiring diagram

*Above right* Scale drawing of one of the 1-12 Class of Roe-bodied Railless trolleybuses. *Terry Russell*

*Right* This wiring diagram for the 67-78 Class of Leyland TB5s reveals that they, along with the later TB7s, were fitted with traction batteries. Clearly shown is the change-over switch between overhead and battery operation, as well as the switch fitted to all BCT trolleybuses that was used when the vehicles were employing a skate in the track. *Courtesy D. F. Potter*

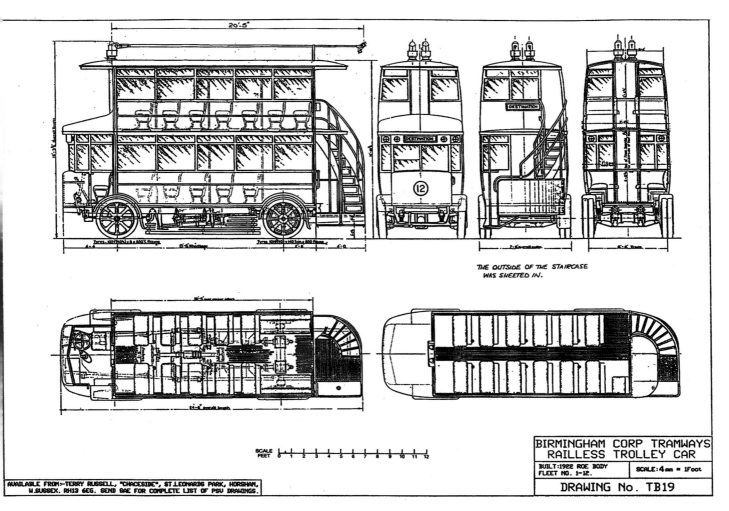

THE OUTSIDE OF THE STAIRCASE
WAS SHEETED IN.

SCALE FEET 0 1 2 3 4 5 6 7 8 9 10 11 12

BIRMINGHAM CORP TRAMWAYS
RAILLESS TROLLEY CAR

BUILT: 1922 ROE BODY
FLEET No. 1-12.

SCALE: 4mm = 1 Foot

DRAWING No. TB19

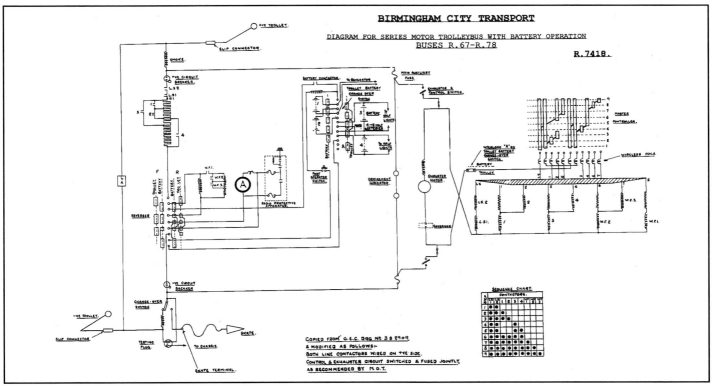

BIRMINGHAM CITY TRANSPORT

DIAGRAM FOR SERIES MOTOR TROLLEYBUS WITH BATTERY OPERATION
BUSES R.67-R.78

R.7418.

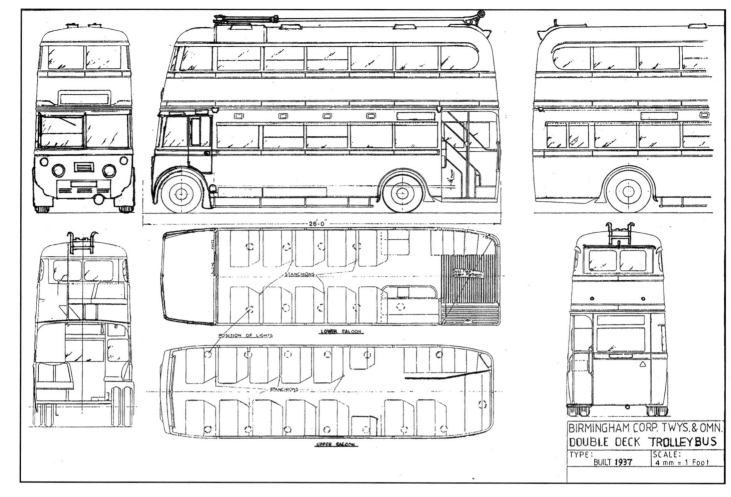

Scale drawing of a Leyland TB5 with an MCCW body from the 67-78 Class. *Author, based on drawing by Terry Russell*

# Depots

## Coventry Road (Arthur Street)

This depot was opened on 24 November 1906 and operated tram services to Yardley and Bordesley Green (later Stechford). From early 1908 until the opening of Highgate Road depot on 25 November 1913 it also operated the Stratford Road tram routes.

The depot was opened for the Yardley trolleybus service on 7 January 1934 and shared its accommodation with the Stechford trams. The trolleybuses occupied rows 1 to 6 adjacent to the main entrance on the north side of the depot, and rows 16 to 19 on the southern side, leaving the middle of the depot to the trams. When those two routes were closed on 2 October 1948 this centre area of the garage was used for parking the new buses.

After the closure of the trolleybus routes on Coventry Road on 30 June 1951 Coventry Road became a bus garage, and passed to the WMPTE on 1 October 1969; it survived until closure in October 1985. The impressive structure still stands at the top of Kingston Hill and is occupied by a company called Light and Sound Design.

## Kyotts Lake Road Works

'The Lake' was opened as a steam tram depot and works by the City of Birmingham Tramways Company in May 1885 and was acquired by the Corporation on 1 January 1907. It was converted to become the tram works in early 1908, and was used for maintaining and overhauling trolleybuses from 1922 to 1929 and after 1934 until the trolleybus closure.

The trolleybuses usually reached the works under their own power with the aid of a skate. From Washwood Heath depot they used the overhead of the 8 and 10 tram routes to get to Dale End and, still using the skate, followed the Albert Street tram and trolleybus routes to Rea Street in Digbeth, before climbing Bradford Street to Camp Hill and thence to the works. At no time did they use trolleybus overhead on these works journeys!

The building was retained for vehicle storage after the final abandonment of the trams in July 1953, and still remains in use divided up into factory units.

## Sampson Road paintshop

This building was opened on leased land in 1925 and was used as the paintshop as there was insufficient space in the nearby Kyotts Lake Road. After the closure of the Stratford Road routes and the gradual run-down of the numbers of tramcars kept in stock, the need for this separate facility became unnecessary and it was used to store all 16 of the Nechells trolleybuses and, for a short time, the first five of the Leyland TTBD2s, from October 1940 until June 1945, when they were sold for scrap. The building was vacated in September 1945.

## Tyburn Road Works

The main bus works, situated on a tram route, was opened in December 1929 and began trolleybus overhauls early in 1930. The trolleybuses were towed all the way from Washwood Heath depot, as although it was situated on a tram track, Tyburn Road was a central reserved track, making operation with the skate impossible! This posed a problem as the very tall trolleybuses would not pass through the doors; they had to have their front axles removed and the vehicles were towed into the works on a small trolley placed at the front of the chassis. Only the Nechells trolleybuses were ever overhauled at Tyburn Road. The Railless trolleybuses received repaints here, which eliminated their cream-painted rocker-panels and gave them a more modern appearance. Trolleybus overhauls ceased in 1933. The works closed in 1995 and was used to store withdrawn buses until it was sold in 1997.

## Washwood Heath

The depot was opened 2 May 1907 and operated the tram services to Washwood Heath, Alum Rock and Nechells. After the conversion of the Nechells route to trolleybus operation on 27 November 1922, the trolleybuses occupied the three roads on the western side of the depot, numbered 7, 8 and 9 and adjacent to the garage offices.

Trolleybuses always drove in and out of Washwood Heath depot yard, but were manoeuvred in the yard with the aid of a reverser and a single piece of tram-line that was used for the skate when the trolleybuses reversed. Access out of the depot to the Nechells route at Bloomsbury Street was always done using the overhead positive tram wire and a return skate attached to the tram track. Trolleybuses needing to visit Kyotts Lake Road Works, however, went all the way to the city centre using the Washwood Heath tram route.

The trolleybus operation was suspended on 30 September 1940, although Leyland TBD1s 4-11 were stored as withdrawn vehicles from 1 March 1940 until the route closure seven months later. After the closure, all the trolleybuses, Leylands 1-11 and AEC 663Ts 12-16 were taken to Sampson Road paintshop and stored until sold for scrap in 1945. After the Washwood Heath and Alum Rock trams were finally abandoned on 1 October 1950 Washwood Heath became a bus garage and passed to the WMPTE on 1 October 1969. It was expanded in the 1980s and still remains open as a Travel West Midlands garage.

## Trolleybus and replacement bus route numbers

### Nechells

| | | |
|---|---|---|
| Trolleybus **7** | | Replaced tram 7 27/10/22. Old Square-Nechells. Closed 30/9/40. |
| Nechells Green | | Short working, 27/10/22. Closed 30/9/40. |
| Bus **43** | | 1/10/40. Old Square-Nechells. |

### Coventry Road

| | | |
|---|---|---|
| Trolleybus **56** | | Replaced tram 56 7/1/34. Albert Street-Hay Mills. Closed 30/6/51. |
| Bus **58A** | | 1/7/51. Albert Street-Hay Mills. |
| Trolleybus **57** | | Replaced tram 57 7/1/34. Station Street-Hay Mills. Closed 29/6/51. |
| Bus **57A** | | 1/7/51. Station Street-Hay Mills. |
| Trolleybus **92** | | Replaced tram 15 7/1/34. Albert Street-Yardley. Closed 30/6/51. |
| Bus **58B** | | 1/7/51. Albert Street-Yardley. |
| Trolleybus **93** | | Replaced tram 16 7/1/34. Station Street-Yardley. Closed 29/6/51. |
| Bus **57B** | | 1/7/51. Station Street-Yardley. |
| Trolleybus **94** | | 5/7/36. Albert Street-Coventry Road (City Boundary). Closed 30/6/51. |
| Bus **58** | | 1/7/51. Albert Street-Sheldon. |
| Trolleybus **95** | | 5/7/36. Station Street-Coventry Road (City Boundary). Closed 29/6/51. |
| No replacement bus route. | | |
| Trolleybus **96** | | 29/10/41. Albert Street-Lode Lane. Closed 30/6/51. |
| Bus **X75** (BMMO) | | Bull Ring-Lode Lane (Rover). |
| Trolleybus **97** | | 29/10/41. Station Street-Lode Lane. Closed 29/6/51. |
| No replacement bus route. | | |
| Trolleybus **98** | | 29/10/41. Coventry Road (City Boundary)-Cattell Road. Closed 30/6/51. |
| Bus to Coventry Road Depot. | | |
| Trolleybus **99** | | 24/1/49. Albert Street-Coventry Road (Wagon Lane). Closed 30/6/51. |
| Bus **58C** | | 1/7/51. Albert Street-Sheldon (Wagon Lane). |
| [Bus **59** | | Albert Street-Lode Lane - not allocated.] |
| Bus **60** | | Albert Street-Cranes Park Estate. |

# Fares and timetables

**Below** An extract from the 1939 *Birmingham Tramway, Omnibus & Street Guide.* It shows that to travel on the 7 route from Old Square to the Nechells terminus cost 2d Ordinary or 1d Children's, while a journey from either Albert Street on a 94 service or Station Street on a 95 service to the terminus at Arden

Oak Road cost 4d Ordinary or 2d Children's. There were in addition a variety of Workmen's tickets ranging from 2d to 5d. The Nechells trolleybus fares were exactly the same in the 1926 edition of the *Guide!*

**Bottom** The 1939 trolleybus timetables published in the *Birmingham Tramway, Omnibus & Street Guide* for the Nechells and Coventry Road routes.

---

### SERVICE No. 7. Nechells.  (TROLLEY 'BUS ROUTE).

**Fares—1d. ORDINARY.**  ½d. CHILDREN'S—BETWEEN.

Old Square and Saltley Rd.—Great Lister St. Junction.
Dartmouth St. and Stuart St.

Saltley Rd.—Great Lister St. Junction and Nechells Terminus.

**FARES—1½d. ORDINARY  2d. WORKMEN'S  1d. CHILDREN'S—BETWEEN**
Old Square and Stuart St.  Dartmouth St. and Nechells Terminus.

**FARES—2d. ORDINARY  3d. WORKMEN'S  1d. CHILDREN'S—BETWEEN**
Old Square and Nechells Terminus

---

### TROLLEY 'BUS SERVICE Nos. 56, 57, 92, 93, 95 and 94.

#### Coventry Road  (Church Road and Arden Oak Road.)

**Fares—1d. ORDINARY.**  ½d. CHILDREN'S—BETWEEN

Albert St. or Station St. and Bordesley Park Rd.
Alcester St. and Muntz St.
Bordesley Park Rd. and Oldknow Rd.
Jenkins St. and Hay Mills Bridge.

Oldknow Rd. and Yardley Rd.
Hay Mills Bridge and Manor House Lane.
Yardley Rd. and Horse Shoes Lane.
Manor House Lane and Wells Rd.
Horse Shoes Lane and Terminus.

**Fares—1½d. ORDINARY  2d. WORKMEN'S  1d. CHILDREN'S—BETWEEN**

Albert St. or Station St. and Muntz St.
Alcester St. and Hay Mills Bridge
Jenkins St. and Yardley Rd.
Oldknow Rd. and Manor House Lane.

Hay Mills Bridge and Horse Shoes Lane
Yardley Rd. and Wells Rd.
Manor House Lane and Terminus.

**Fares—2d. ORDINARY  3d. WORKMEN'S  1d. CHILDREN'S—BETWEEN.**

Albert St. or Station St. and Hay Mills Bridge
Alcester St. and Yardley Rd.
Jenkins St. and Manor House Lane.

Oldknow Rd. and Horse Shoes Lane
Hay Mills Bridge and Wells Rd.
Yardley Rd. and Terminus

**Fares—2½d. ORDINARY  4d. WORKMEN'S  1d. CHILDREN'S—BETWEEN**

Albert St. or Station St. and Yardley Rd.
Alcester St. and Manor House Lane

Jenkins St. and Horse Shoes Lane.
Oldknow Rd. and Terminus

**Fares—3d. ORDINARY.  4d. WORKMEN'S  1½d. CHILDREN'S—BETWEEN**

Albert St. or Station St. and Manor House La.  Alcester St. and Wells Rd.
Jenkins St. and Terminus.

**Fares—3½d. ORDINARY.  5d. WORKMEN'S  1½d. CHILDREN'S—BETWEEN.**

Albert St. or Station St. and Wells Rd.  Alcester St. and Terminus.

**Fares—4d. ORDINARY  5d. WORKMEN'S  2d. CHILDREN'S—BETWEEN.**

Albert St or Station St and Terminus

---

### FIRST AND LAST TROLLEY BUS SERVICES TO AND FROM CITY.

| No. | Termini | WEEKDAYS To City First Bus am | To City Last Bus pm | From City First Bus am | From City Last Bus pm | SUNDAYS To City First Bus am | To City Last Bus pm | From City First Bus am | From City Last Bus pm |
|---|---|---|---|---|---|---|---|---|---|
| 7 | Nechells and Old Square ... ... | 5 13 | 1114 | 5 28 | 1130 | 8 58 | 1114 | 9 13 | 1130 |
| 56 | Hay Mills and Albert Street ... ... | 4 58 | 1111 | 5 18 | 1130 | 8 53 | 1111 | 9 12 | 1130 |
| 57 | Hay Mills and Station Street ... ... | 5 3 | 11 9 | 5 28 | 1130 | 8 49 | 11 9 | 9 8 | 1130 |
| 92 | Yardley and Albert Street ... ... | 5 31 | 11 6 | 5 53 | 1130 | 8 48 | 11 6 | 9 12 | 1130 |
| 93 | Yardley and Station Street ... ... | 4 58 | 11 4 | 5 28 | 11 0 | 8 44 | 11 4 | 9 8 | 1130 |
| 94 | Coventry Road (City Boundary) and Albert Street | 5 23 | 1055 | 5 53 | 1130 | 8 37 | 1055 | 9 12 | 1130 |

# Tickets

Throughout the operational life of Birmingham's trolleybuses, only the Bell Punch system was used. The conductor carried a Bell Punch machine, a satchel and a rack of tickets.

Most of the tickets were printed by the Bell Punch Company, but in 1934 the Department borrowed a Chambon ticket printing machine. In April 1935 this machine was purchased and was used to print all the Corporation's 1d Ordinary tickets as well as small batches of 1½d Ordinary and 2½d Ordinary tickets. Some of these pre-war 1d tickets and limited numbers of the 1½d tickets were printed on this Chambon machine with the legend 'Birmingham City Transport'.

The last fare increase that affected the trolleybuses was that of 1949. This increased the price of a journey from the city to the terminus to 5d. As a result the trolleybus

conductors had to carry ticket denominations ranging from ½d to 2d Children's, 1d to 5d Ordinary and 3d to 8d Workmen's and Exchange.

All the titles of the undertaking were used on the Bell Punch Company tickets. 'Birmingham Corporation Tramways' was used until October 1927, when it was replaced by 'Birmingham Corporation Tramways and Omnibus Department'. The change of name in November 1937 did not alter the name of the undertaking on the tickets, except on some Chambon tickets, until July 1949, when the correct title of 'Birmingham City' was printed on the tickets. The conversion to Ultimate machines and tickets did not occur on Coventry Road until after the abandonment of the trolleybuses.

The tickets shown below are a selection of those that would have been in use on the BCT trams and buses, as well as Birmingham's trolleybus routes from 1922 until 1951.

½d Children's, Bell Punch, BCTOD

1d Ordinary, Chambon, BCTOD

1d Children's, Bell Punch, BCT

1½d Ordinary, Chambon, BCT

1½d Children's, Bell Punch, BCTOD

2d Ordinary, Bell Punch, Tramways (Nechells)

2d Ordinary, Bell Punch, BCTOD

2d Children's, Bell Punch, BCT

2½d Ordinary, Chambon,
BCTOD

3d Ordinary, Bell Punch,
BCT

3d Exchange, Bell Punch,
BCTOD

3d Workmen's, Bell Punch,
BCTOD

3½d Ordinary, Bell Punch,
BCT

4d Ordinary, Bell Punch,
BCTOD

4d Exchange, Bell Punch,
BCTOD

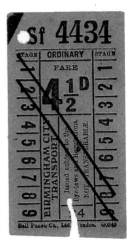

4½d Ordinary, Bell Punch,
BCT

5d Ordinary, Bell Punch,
BCTOD

5d Workmen's, Bell Punch,
BCT

5d Exchange, Bell Punch,
BCTOD

6d Workmen's, Bell Punch,
BCT

**7d Workmen's, Bell Punch, BCT**

**7d Exchange, Bell Punch, BCT**

**8d Workmen's, Bell Punch, BCT**

**8d Exchange, Bell Punch, BCT**

**6d Night Service, Bell Punch, BCT**

**10d Football Return, Bell Punch, BCTOD**

# What might have been

If the trolleybus system had survived the decimation of electric traction in the city, the Corporation would have required replacement trolleybuses in the early 1950s. The only available four-wheeled trolleybus chassis available were the BUT 9611T and the Sunbeam F4. As BCT had always ordered Leyland trolleybuses before the war, then almost certainly they would have favoured the BUT chassis. The bodies would have followed pre-war practice and been built by Metro-Cammell (or possibly Crossley Motors) to the current, albeit modified, bus body designs.

The accompanying drawing shows what 'trolleybus 91' might have looked like. *D. R. Harvey*